Praise for *Let It Begin With Me*

Mindy's clear spirit shines through in each of her interviews as she draws out wisdom and practical suggestions for the task of establishing peace in the world. It is important to be both inspired and equipped in order to take the next step in each of our lives and make this a better place for all. Mindy has done both in this fabulous book!

> —Scott C. Miller, author of *Until It's Gone: Ending Poverty in Our Nation, in Our Lifetime* and co-founder of the Circles campaign, *www.movethemountain.org*

In Let It Begin With Me, *Mindy draws upon the wisdom of "peacebuilders" and challenges all of us to not only reflect upon the possibility of peace, but to also take inspired action in making peace a reality in our world.*

> —Rev. Robin Haruna, The Peace Rock Project, *www.peacerocks.org*

This book is a stand for people being their absolute best. Let It Begin With Me *shows us how "being our best" creates peace from within. And when we have peace within, we take another step closer to peace for all.*

> —Vicki Abadesco, director of Soul Shoppe's Student Peacemaker Programs and creator of "The Peace Path" Conflict Resolution Tools for Schools, *www.soulshoppe.com*

The contributors to this book are peace teachers who have arrived to carry out the most important mission on earth. Their evolutionary thinking on peace feeds our heart's longing for a better world while evoking the power within us to achieve it.

—Rita Marie Johnson, creator of BePeace and founding director of Rasur Foundation International

Let It Begin With Me

21 Voices of the New Peace Movement

ALSO BY THE AUTHOR

What If It All Goes Right? Creating a New World
of Peace, Prosperity and Possibility
(Morgan James Publishing, 2010)

Let It Begin With Me

21 Voices of the New
Peace Movement

Mindy Audlin

Featuring Interviews With

His Holiness Karma Kuchen Rinpoche, Barbara Marx
Hubbard, Joe Vitale, Lisa Nichols, Dr. John Demartini, Edgar
Mitchell, B.J. Dohrmann, Howard Martin, Stephen Dinan, Jim
Bunch, James Trapp, Garland Landrith and more

uniTy®
Books
Unity Village, Missouri

Let It Begin With Me
First Edition 2011

Unity Books titles are available at special discounts for bulk purchases for study groups, book clubs, sales promotions, book signings or fundraising. To place an order, call the Unity Customer Care Department at 1-866-236-3571 or email *wholesaleaccts@unityonline.org.*

Cover design: Unity Artists

Interior design: The Covington Group, Kansas City, Missouri

Library of Congress Control Number: 2010933801
ISBN: 978-0-87159-353-5
Canada BN 13252 0933 RT

*This book is dedicated to every man, woman and child
who stands for peace in the presence of conflict; for
love in the presence of hatred; and for forgiveness in
the presence of injury.*

"Blessed are the peacemakers, for they shall be
called children of God."

—Matthew 5:9

Contents

INTRODUCTION

My passion and purpose revolve around the bringing forth of possibility. What better playground than the Global Peace Movement that is taking shape this very moment around the planet?

The goal of world peace is nothing new. But what does "world peace" mean? What does it look like? Is it really possible? If we set such a goal, what could we create?

In an attempt to explore these questions, I decided to ask some visionaries: How do you set a goal for something the world has never seen before?

In the course of 12 weeks, my weekly *Leading Edge* radio program on Unity Online Radio took the issue to heart. Each interview was lovingly transcribed and edited for print, resulting in the present book, *Let It Begin With Me.* What you have here are 21 thought-provoking dialogues focused on how each of us can do our part to bring about a more peace-filled world.

In these pages, we delve into the most important questions facing humanity: What does it mean to be a peacebuilder? Why should we care? Where do we start?

Together we explore both practical and theoretical solutions, leading the way for people in all walks of life to join in a movement that is transforming the planet. We conclude each interview with a series of questions and reflection points to allow you to contemplate each message more deeply and take your own inspired actions for building peace in your life and in the world.

In the words of Summer of Peace organizer Stephen Dinan, "Ours is the generation. And *now* is the time."

Peace …

Reflection Points

What does *peace* mean to you?

What do you think it means to be a "peacebuilder"?

1

START WITH THE HEART

Howard Martin

We've often heard the song "Let There be Peace on Earth," which opens with these words: "Let there be peace on Earth, and let it begin with me." To capture the depth and meaning of this phrase, and to more fully understand through a scientific lens how to make this happen, I talked with Howard Martin from the Institute of HeartMath. The Institute's scientific studies of the human heart, the relationship between mind and emotions, and the quest to consciously create a state of "coherence" demonstrate the enormous potential for real world impact based on the efforts of each of us as individuals.

> "By regulating our emotions through the power of the heart, we begin to set up a different energetic momentum in our life that begins to attract new opportunities."
>
> —Howard Martin, the Institute of HeartMath

Q: *HeartMath is a powerful tool for anyone who is serious about their spiritual journey. Tell us a little about what HeartMath is.*

HeartMath is, first of all, the name of our organization. But more important, it is a system of techniques, tools and very interesting concepts, all underpinned by scientific research, designed to promote heart-based living to put us more in touch with this Magnificent Intelligence we have that has been called "the heart" for thousands of years. We apply it to our daily lives where it is needed the most.

Q: *Why is this so important?*

I think we are in a major shift period right now. It seems we are in a time period when we are making choices now that have dynamic impact on our near-term and long-term future. There is a lot of newness in the air and there is a tremendous amount of chaos also taking place. We can see that depicted across the world stage very easily.

The transition is happening very quickly. The speed of change is accelerating. It is ramping up dramatically. In the process, most systems that provide the structure of modern life are coming under a lot of stress and beginning to show that they are not as effective anymore. These systems underpin the security that we have had for a long time, which creates a lot of angst, insecurity and uncertainty in people.

At the same time, there are so many new and exciting things that are happening in the world today, so many people who are moving into new states of consciousness. As a result, they are coming up with more creative ways of creating harmony, and new ways in which the world functions are emerging that we've never had before.

We are moving somewhere now that we have never been and therefore it is hard to predict. In the midst of all that, I think one of the things we are seeing is the emergence of the heart's intelligence.

Q: *You talk about the "intelligence" of the heart. A lot of us think of the brain as being the center of intelligence. So what is "heart's intelligence"? What does that mean?*

Research right now is showing that intelligence in many ways is distributed throughout the entire body. When I talk about heart intelligence, I am not just talking about the physical heart. I am talking about this part of us, this intelligence that is high-speed and intuitive.

It is the type of intelligence that gives us the power to do what we usually cannot. It is an intelligence that looks after the whole. It looks out for more than just the self-serving interest that we often have from just our logical, linear intelligence. It is an amazing intelligence that gives us the ability to make decisions big and small as we play the game of life.

To me, it is our own best friend and most reliable guide. It is an intelligence that has been talked about for thousands of years. As a matter of fact, the earliest writings I have seen about the heart being intelligent go back 4,500 years to ancient Chinese medicine.

I believe that spirit integrates humanness through the heart and through the qualities associated with the heart. It enters into us, into our consciousness, into what drives our thoughts, our actions and our reactions. It comes in through the heart level, through the emotions that are often associated metaphorically with the heart, like love.

Q: *I know much of the work you do at HeartMath is about reducing stress. It is about coming into what you call coherence. Talk about coherence. What does it mean to be coherent?*

Coherence is a state where less energy is being wasted. It is a state where all of our systems are working together in harmony at the physiological level and the psychological level. The medical term for it is *psycho-physiological coherence*, which means both physical and psychological. It is a state where we are able to experience positive emotions more easily, like love, care, compassion and nonjudgment appreciation.

It is a state where all the biological systems are synchronized to the heart. That means things like digestion, respiration, hormonal release, immune system response. In that state we become very aware.

You can get to coherence through meditation and prayer, but it is not a state where you have to be in meditation or prayer to experience it. You can be right in the midst of your daily activity and in that state you are more perceptive: What are you really feeling? What are you really thinking? What are you perceiving?

You are also more sensitive to the environment around you, to people, to the actual physical environment that you are in. So it is a very interesting high-performance state that is useful in things like business, for example, not just in spiritual practice. It is a physiological state that can be measured through our technology, measuring changes in the heart's rhythms that reflect coherence within the body.

Q: Howard, what does peace mean to you?

Peace means people cooperating more, working together more. It is more of a harmonious relationship with people. It has a lot less judgment in it, for starters, where some of the differences are not as pronounced, where people are seeing each other for who they are, whether it is between countries or regions around the world or individuals in their homes, in their workplaces.

Peace is where there is less friction and less tension, more flexibility, more live-and-let-live and especially more support for one another. I think that it starts with the individual.

You have to have peace inside yourself before you can really offer much peace to others. So it is an individual job and I think that it is important to make that point even if most people already recognize that.

But then it goes into our relationships, not just to world peace and all that, but how we are treating others. How do we treat others at work, how do we treat others in our families? When we are out in the world, how do we treat waiters in a restaurant? Do we put that extra love and care for these people? Do we really make an effort to listen to them, to understand them, to really get a sense of who these folks are, what is meaningful to them in their lives and then what do we do about that?

Once we understand that, do we make an effort to support them? As we spread that, it goes far beyond the individual in the home, in the workplaces into an overall sort of energetic environment that allows for differences and allows for the practical approach to peace. There are going to be conflicts. There are going to be things that come up. But then how do we resolve them, individually or nationalistically?

I think it is a process. I think peace is unfolding. More people want it. They want less tension between individuals and organizations and nations, et cetera. It is a stepping-stone process. It has to be worked at, and I think that's important for everybody to understand. But peace takes a little time. It certainly takes patience and it certainly takes practical applications from the heart to make that happen.

Q: *What are some of the things that you do in your own spiritual practice to cultivate peace, to cultivate harmony?*

For me, it is a self-observation of where my internal pitch is—meaning whether my attitudes and perceptions are on the upside or on the downside. What am I really seeing? Am I complaining and griping about things, about the workload, about what I have to do, about the last phone call that did not go well? Or am I taking it on the up slant. That is one place to look.

The other place for me that is very important is *judgment*. Judgment is the antithesis of peace in many ways. We live in a world where judgment is the international sport. Who can out-judge the other, who can find fault more quickly and more creatively and even more humorously?

I look at where my judgments are about people, places, things and issues. I try to replace those judgments with more care or more appreciation. That is one major important thing that I do.

Another one worth mentioning: *care*. Really put out more care, not just to wait for situations in life to evoke care, but really put it out and use the time between doing things to be conscious of putting out more care. There are times when I am driving in my car, there are times when I am walking through the offices to go from one place to the other for a meeting. I can slow the rambling mind down a little bit, focus on the heart in those situations, rather than planning out the next thing. I put out more care and make that a conscious practice. All these things add up.

You have to break the mechanics of normal thought processes. Certainly I make mistakes and I stumble and I say things I should not say and I have attitudes that I really wish I did not have. All those things come up. When they do, I go back to working on one of the primary judgments that permeates the world, and that is self-judgment.

I try to show myself a little more compassion about what is going on in my life, because life is life. We all have our ups and downs.

Q: *Peace begins with us and so does love and so does compassion. Everything I am hearing you say really speaks to that journey from the head to the heart, from judgment to caring. How does HeartMath help us live a heart-based life?*

We have developed lots of new angles and understandings about the heart and about emotions and things like that. A lot of our focus is on learning to regulate emotion, which is done through the power of the heart.

Regulating emotion does not mean suppressing emotion, but it does mean using your maturity and the power of your consciousness to make emotional choices that are regenerative. To me this is often a missing step in spiritual practice.

Q: *What is the impact when we shift the coherence level of our heart? What are the repercussions of that?*

First there is a physical impact, a health impact. When we make a shift emotionally, for example, we will say we are feeling happy, and then we get some news and we go to sad. We are the opposite of that. When those things occur, about 1,400 biochemical changes instantly go off in our body.

So we are really our own pharmacists in a way because we are calling the shots on the hormonal releases that go on in our system depending on what we are feeling.

There are physiological factors that affect the nervous system, the physical heart. They also have an effect on the brain. A lot of that effect comes from the heart, and the signals going from heart back to brain change, depending upon how coherent we are and what we do with our emotions.

Beyond that there is the impact of perception. When we are operating in a less than desirable emotional state, our perceptions begin to shut down. It narrows our focus. We are not really seeing the big picture. We do not really see the things in life that we can appreciate. It begins to color our overall perceptions of the world. In other words, we begin to magnetize other things into our life, the holographic choices that we make begin to dictate what occurs in our life.

Q: That sounds a lot like the Law of Attraction.

In a sense, yes. We are making these choices emotionally, not just mentally deciding what we want. It is the feelings and the emotions that support what we decide. It makes all the difference in the world.

So by adjusting your emotions, by regulating your emotions through the power of the heart and HeartMath techniques, we begin to set up a different energetic momentum in our life that begins to attract new opportunities and new things. It has a practical side to it.

We make a clear point that we have all got the things we need to go through and to learn from, but we have the ability to co-create and create new things in our life, but it is not necessarily just thinking it will happen.

Q: Right. The feeling aspect is an important part of that equation. What is the impact when you bring people together—which HeartMath does—so they are more and more coherent? What is the impact of having masses of people aligned in a heart-centered life?

Let me say this first: The journey from the head to the heart can be a long journey. But I think it is going to get easier. Everybody is talking about the shift, and what is the shift?

I think part of the shift is the emergence of easier access to the heart's intelligence. I see examples of it already. For instance, I see things that have worked in the past, that have been cornerstones of how the world operates, are not working as well as before right now, are not rewarding in the same way.

One of those would be ambition ... going for what you want just for yourself without regard for others. Using ambition to get what you want has worked a lot throughout the history of humankind, and it has helped build the world we have today. But I do not see it rewarding in the same way right now. It is just not getting the same result. In many cases, it creates the opposite effect.

Here's another thing that I see happening: You know how a lot of times people that have come from the heart, who have been more involved in the softer side of things or spiritual approaches to things, seem to get the short end of the stick?

I see that changing. I see more reward coming back for that now than before. So there are changes that are going to be occurring in how we operate, as the shift unfolds. Access to the heart and actually putting importance on the heart and more heart-directed and heart-based living is a part of what is occurring in the shift.

The outplay of that will take time. I do not have a crystal ball to predict what's going to happen or by when, and I think that's fun because we cannot see what is coming. As I said in the beginning, what is emerging is something we have never experienced as a global species before. So the only way we can try to see it now is to try to take what we have today and ramp it up some. It would be kind of like someone who is driving a horse and buggy that thinks the next mode of transportation is going to be a better buggy. They cannot see an airplane yet.

Q: Things are changing so rapidly today through technology that who knows what that next buggy is going to be!

That is right. If you know this or believe this, it will bring in a new intelligence that will give us the ability to come up with more creative and effective solutions to many of these problems we face in the world today. Things can look hopeless, it can look like, "Hey, game is over. We have messed up this plan so bad we are never going to get out of it." I can have those feelings. But I do not think it is true.

I think we are going to find ways to meet these challenges, and yes there are going to be things we have to go through and that the world has to go through. There has been a lot of density built up in this world for a very long time, and that is going to be accounted for in some way. Things have to go down in a certain way to sort of balance out the energetic scales. But in the process, I believe we will come into this new intelligence that gives us the ability to come up with the solutions we need for problems that look almost insurmountable today. So I am very hopeful about that.

Q: Jack Canfield says the Global Coherence Initiative is "perhaps the greatest experiment in the history of the world." What is the Global Coherence Initiative?

We have always believed that changing consciousness needs to precede the changes in action. Activity that occurs in the world comes from people, of course, doing what they do inside. When consciousness itself begins to change, then mass consciousness begins to change in daily activity.

The Global Coherence Initiative is a top-down approach. How do we affect consciousness itself? We believe that mass human emotion, whether positive or negative, has an impact on the consciousness climate and that we all begin to feel and sense things collectively.

Not only that. We believe mass human emotion can have a measurable impact on the actual planet itself. So the project has several facets to it. First of all, we formed this membership that you can access through the Global Coherence Initiative website (*www.glcoherence.org*) and membership is free.

There are webinars and events that we do all the time for members only. We also have care focus emails that we send out regularly when there is a particular planetary need. We send messages asking all the members to start using their heart-focused caring intention through meditation, prayers, affirmations or whatever people do to help ease a certain situation or to help something where the world is in need.

On the site you can access the Care Focus Room. It is an amazing place where you see this globe, and when you go into this room, it marks your location on the globe so you can see people all around the world who are there together with you at the same time. As of today, we have more than 16,000 members, and those are solid members operating as a coherent group, and they are from all over the world. There are 73 countries represented in that 16,000 people. So it has truly become global. We've also added science to it because that is part of what HeartMath does.

The purpose of the membership is to engender individual and collective coherence, to help the individuals become more coherent themselves and then to keep that group organized in a coherent way so that the collective power can be utilized for the betterment of the world.

Q: And you are tracking all this, so there is data showing the impact of the collective coherence. What are you seeing?

That is the science part of it. We have developed a technology that has the ability to measure changes in the earth's geomagnetic field and another field associated with that field called the ionosphere, both of which are part of the earth's living systems. They are the fields surrounding the earth that protect us from solar radiation and things like that.

Our hypothesis is that those fields can be impacted by mass human emotion, and the technology we have developed allows us to study those fields and monitor those fields and really dig in and begin to understand what goes on in those fields relative to what changes are occurring in society.

We have one functional sensor site set up in northern California, where we are located, that is feeding information as we are talking right now back into the Institute of HeartMath research labs. You can see an update of that information daily on the Global Coherence Initiative website. We are looking at these changes in the planetary fields.

Our researchers are really professionals, so we are very careful not to get involved in phenomenalistic claims. We are building this on a very, very solid, academically based research platform. So we take it slowly, in steps. We are not making any claims about what consciousness is doing to those fields yet, because we are really only beginning to understand these fields better.

We are going to place more of these sensors around the world, and the technology to link these together is being developed now. We will have between 12 and 15 of these sensor sites located strategically around the world, which will give us a land-based picture of the geomagnetic field and the ionosphere.

We will correlate our data with data coming in from space weather satellites that are run by the U.S. government and begin to get a really clear picture of these fields. As that system is developed, we will do experiments and we will bring together the Global Coherence Initiative community. We will increase the coherence individually and collectively and focus on various planetary situations and needs. Ultimately we hope that we can actually see a change in these geomagnetic fields as a result of that.

So here is the slam dunk of this whole thing. This is why Jack Canfield made a statement about this being perhaps the greatest experiment in the history of the world. What if we bring the group together in a coherent state and we are able to monitor and measure that group coherence? We will be able to do that in a not-too-distant future through web-based applications.

We focus on a planetary need and then we are able to detect a change in the geomagnetic and ionospheric fields. Then we link that change to something that occurs in a positive way in society. That would provide some solid, empirical proof for the first time that our collective energetic fields, our thoughts and our feelings and our prayers and our meditations actually do have an impact. That they actually work.

Maybe we do not need that because we have believed that for thousands of years. But there is something about proof that adds potency to belief.

And if we can prove that, it will prove something that we have never had proof of in the history of mankind yet we have always believed. That would be revolutionary.

Q: *Howard, if you could share a single message with us as individuals in a global community dedicated to bringing forth peace, what would be the message that you would want us to take away?*

What you could take away would be this: Within every person there is an organizing and central intelligence that really can and does lift us beyond our problems. It is there all the time; it never goes away.

Sometimes we go away from it. It is called heart, and no matter what comes up in your life, you have got this power inside. You have your own source of security and intelligence to give you the guidance you need with whatever comes up, and it is through accessing this guidance that you will come out with a new understanding of yourself and of the world. It will give you the power to actually make a difference in the world.

*****

Howard Martin has more than 30 years of experience in business and personal development as the executive vice president of HeartMath (*www.heartmath.com*), a systematic approach to developing the intelligence of the heart. He is the co-author of *The HeartMath Solution.* You can learn about the Global Coherence Initiative at *www.glcoherence.org* as well as on Facebook.

*****

Reflection Points

What are some ways you listen to the "intelligence of the heart"? What intuitive guidance is your heart providing for you now in your life?

Howard expounds on a state of "coherence." In addition to prayer and meditation, what are some ways you can consciously remind yourself to "get coherent" when stressful situations arise in your life?

The Peacebuilder Challenge

Visit the HeartMath website at *www.heartmath.org* and sign up for its free resources. Use the free "Personal Tracker" web application each day for at least 30 days to become more conscious of your own personal coherence level as you strive to be more heart-focused in your daily routines.

2

EVOLUTION TO PEACE

Barbara Marx Hubbard, Carolyn Anderson and
John Zwerver

*Humanity is evolving into a conscious awareness of our connection as
a global family. At the forefront of this great shift is futurist Barbara
Marx Hubbard, founder of the Foundation for Conscious Evolution.*

*Buckminster Fuller has called Barbara "the best informed human now
alive regarding futurism and the foresights it has produced." Widely
regarded as his philosophical heir, Barbara is a social innovator,
speaker, author, educator and leader in the new worldview of conscious evolution.*

*Barbara joined me for a round table discussion on the shift we are
experiencing worldwide, along with Carolyn Anderson and John
Zwerver, founders of Global Family, an international network of individuals and groups who recognize our interconnectedness as one
human family.*

> "Evolutionary spirituality leads you into co-creating a
> world, and then it feeds back into your own self-
> evolution."
>
> —Barbara Marx Hubbard, founder of the Foundation
> for Conscious Evolution

Q: *I want to ask each of you this question, and I'll begin with you, Barbara. What does peace mean to you and how does humanity ascend to the consciousness and manifestation of peace?*

Barbara: I believe that peace is a by-product of co-creation, and that it's not a goal any more than health is a goal. The feelings of peace for me come from two things: the connection with Source and co-creation in a way that the creativity of several of us is sustainable. I'm also realizing that to have a sustainable sense of this, you'll need a sustainable field, and by that I mean two or more and eventually many, many more who are sustaining this consciousness themselves together.

John: It's interesting. When you go to the dictionary and look up the word *peace*, the focus is so much about the absence of hostility, conflict or active aggression between nations and competing groups. Peace is our natural state of being if we're in alignment with Source. If we're in a supported field and if we're actually doing the things that we're being called to do in this lifetime, then we are at peace.

It's a state of being. It's presence. It's stillness living in us, through us. This is a natural state, and when we're not at peace, when we realize that we are in conflict or in some kind of confusion, then it's important to check back in and say, "What's going on here? What is it that is impacting me in a way that deviates from that being of peacefulness?"

Carolyn: Recently I was reading a book by Dr. David Hawkins, *The Eye of the I*, and he calibrates different states of being. Hawkins says that peace is actually a higher state of consciousness than either unconditional love or joy. It's right below enlightenment in his calibration system.

So I feel that it is our basic nature and it is an actual frequency. It's an attractor field that is our nature emanating from us when we are aligned with our true nature.

Q: Barbara, given what Carolyn just said, how is it that we've gotten so off-track? There seems to be a lot of violence happening on our planet right now.

Barbara: When you look at nature, violence is everywhere and it's never considered bad. Other species are eating each other alive and there are roots of trees that are fighting so they can get the sunlight—it's the way nature has survived.

What is amazing to me is when the species called *human* suddenly says, "Don't kill. Treat others as yourself, no matter who they are. Love your enemy as yourself." That is really an evolution of the species within itself.

What I am really noticing is the number, hundreds of thousands, millions of people who are shifting. I would say it's a species evolution—not only the human species, but nature's species that would now be designed not to kill, but to cooperate and to consciously seek a state of peace, enlightenment and love as a goal of life.

You have to look at it with evolutionary eyes, and then you say not so much what went wrong, but "What's going right?" In the light of our violence, what's going right becomes more important.

Q: That's a great way of looking at it. As you said, there is violence in nature. If we want to evolve, what does that mean for our vision of peace?

John: It seems to me that although we see this evolution going on in nature and obviously it impacts us as human beings, the transition that we're going through at the moment is fed by fear.

I was reading something the other day about weapons of mass destruction, and to me, the greatest weapon of mass destruction is not a bomb or some man-made disease. It's this ever-growing state of fear and antagonism that's created because of the unknown.

In this transition, there is a lot of fear. It's magnified by individuals and groups who choose to play on that fear and foster dissension, separation, hatred and all of these things—sometimes subtle and sometimes in more fanatical forms. I think a lot of what goes on right now is this sense of fear because we are in transition.

Barbara: John, it's also true that there is a spread of empathy along with the fear. It's amazing how much empathy there is.

I think a fundamental cause of the lack of peace we experience in our world is the sense of separation that exists between human beings. When we don't feel connected to our Source and we don't feel connected to one another, then it's easy to project "enemy" on one another.

Of course, this is happening at the international level, in the national community, and within our own families. A very profound healing happens when we do feel connected. We feel, "I am a universal being, I am a God being in human form and I'm connected to all life."

That begins to heal the sense of separation and create a feeling of peace. When you realize that we now can see Earth as one body, for all the violence and fear that exists, there is a dawning awareness that we are all members of planet Earth.

It's really interesting that a crisis like global warming might be a vital factor for peace, because it forces us to realize that we have to not only cooperate but change certain behavior patterns at a very deep level in order to survive.

Q: *And at a collective level, at a global-family level.*

Barbara: It has to be collective. It isn't enough for each individual to do a little something better. Therefore we're being forced into a collective consciousness to survive—a global collective, not just tribal collective.

Q: So, how do we make that shift? That's a big shift for humanity.

Barbara: It sure is. It's all about survival, as evidently most people won't do it out of empathy. Some will, but the rest might do it because they want to stay above water.

We've already had a number of collective experiences. In the United States we had Katrina. We had 9/11. We had the passings of Princess Diana and Michael Jackson, which really brought the whole world together as one. There were more than a billion people who watched the memorial service for Michael Jackson and had some open-heartedness during that period of time. Just think of what that means. That's almost a sixth of humanity.

Q: We're talking about the collective consciousness, so what is the role of the individual in creating this shift?

Barbara: Obviously the individual is the point of contact of Source and life itself, so there's a very deep path for an individual human to become resonant with—an inner connection to the whole and the inner relationship with one another.

In every religion, whether you are in Kabbalah, Buddhism or Mystic Christianity, there is quite a long and deep path that leads up to the fulfillment of that religion. But to lead up to the fulfillment of yourself as a co-creative, universal human on a planet undergoing a crisis, you can't look to those old paths as sufficient.

That's a new type of human or mass, and the co-creator would be one who is incarnating the creative process, expressing it, joining with others not just as a mystic or a cooperator, but as a co-creator.

That's again giving humanity a sense of how challenging it is to do something that's new without there being a leader, a church, or a particular teaching that everybody could follow.

I'm very sympathetic with us as a species. No species had to go through this consciously, and know they would do it or become extinct.

Carolyn: The essential shift to create peace on Earth, of course, starts with individuals. That's where it begins, because the outer is strictly a reflection of the inner. It's that shift from ego to essence that Barbara wrote about in her book *Emergence*.

I've been doing personal work literally for decades, and when that shift occurs, it's monumental. What it has created in my life has been a feeling of harmony and resonance, moment by moment, day by day. Not that I don't slip, but that the ground of my being is different from where it was, say, 10 years ago.

One element of peace on Earth is right relationship with service and with our creative energy when we are aligned with what we are here to do, giving our gifts and our talents. That certainly supports peace in our lives, and it contributes to peace on Earth because I feel that each of us is an element of that whole. When we ourselves are whole, giving our unique gifts, that does shift the entire field.

Q: Yes. Barbara, you talked about evolutionary spirituality, which is also being called "the inner big bang." What is evolutionary spirituality and how does it help create peace on the planet?

Barbara: It's incarnating the impulse of evolution as your own desire to create. It's aligning the essence of your being with the core of the evolutionary spiral, which you could call Designing Intelligence, God Force, Consciousness, Implicate Order.

It's aligning that inner aspect of your being that wants to grow, to evolve and to connect with the power of the process of creation itself. When you are in full evolutionary spirituality, you and that impulse of creation are one. Evolutionary spirituality entails an identification with the unfolding process of creation, which is now localized as your vocation, your calling, your expression. When you say "yes" to that, you enter the path of the co-creator.

John: I think the question that then exists is "How does this happen for the individual, this sense of self-awareness—this awareness that we're becoming something different than what we have been, that we're shifting to a new way of being? How does that self-awareness then lead into full self-expression?"

It's one thing to say, "We're co-creators. We're being called to be out there in the world. We're being called to be peacemakers," or whatever our calling is. But how do you do that in full self-expression with every part of your being, knowing that we are going through this shift from ego to essence, in harmony and resonance with the co-creative expression?

We know that happens in a field. We know that to fully be a co-creator, you want to be surrounded by people who share those values and those initiatives, but how do you do that?

What does it mean to people in their lives to be able to take this and then say, "Yes, I understand this. I feel this. I know in my life something is being called forth. I'm not quite sure what it is, but I'm sure it's not more of the same. How do I go about doing that?"

Barbara: John, because it's such an unfolding process, people need a sustainable field in which that can unfold, because it's very much like the growth of a newborn baby. There's no way that you can get it to get up and walk the next day.

Let's assume we are a newborn, evolutionary, universal human and we get a taste of our own potential. I need something for myself, and I feel it's coming forth. Then I can't quite sustain it or build on it. Then the next spark will come and there's no older parent who knows what I'm going through. There may be some peers who know it because they're going through it too, but there's no grown-up human somewhere who has been through this whole thing and knows how a planet evolves.

Q: Barbara, you were nominated as a vice-presidential candidate back in 1984. You ran on the platform of the vision that you held for a Peace Room. Talk about what the Peace Room is, and how that vision has grown and manifested.

Barbara: It was and is a great vision that we need a function as sophisticated as our war rooms, which map and track every enemy and how to kill them. The Peace Room maps, tracks and connects what's working, what's emergent, what's creative and communicates what's working in America and the world.

I was able to get 200 delegates to sign a petition to place my name in nomination for vice president. Our goal was for me to be able to declare this at a convention. I didn't have as my goal to be vice president. But if that had happened, I would have created this function.

This was before the Internet had spread. Now the social networks and the Internet are maturing every day. Everybody who wants to communicate now can communicate with somebody, somehow, whether it's through Twitter, Facebook or YouTube.

The global emergences are in every field and function, the innovative and creative solutions. The word *emergence* is very powerful these days, and I think it's a very good word. Connecting what's emergent leads to convergence.

Q: Yes, that's exciting. For a moment, let's step into the shoes of the average American husband/wife, father/mother trying to pay bills, wanting to provide for their families, trying to balance work responsibilities, all those things that we deal with in life. Why should the average person care about conscious evolution or even a peacebuilding movement like the work that we're doing?

John: I think that's a really important question, because it's one thing for us to be talking about these concepts that may seem to the average person to be far removed from their daily wants and needs. But the reality is that within our hearts and within our souls, we are all striving for and have this desire for this inner peace and this sense of connectedness that we've been talking about.

The reality, I think, is that people are searching for answers. They're searching for something beyond the daily issue of feeding their kids and making the mortgage payments because they know that that isn't the end-all on the deal. That's what's in front of them at the moment, but they also realize that this is part of a much bigger issue, a much bigger picture in their life.

People are searching. They're searching for it in spiritual community. They're searching for it back in the churches, and especially in places where the search is beyond the traditional dogma.

There's a mystical kind of aspect to this, for many people these days, that is kind of interesting. It's one thing to have this experience within oneself. It's another thing to step outside the cave and to say, "What is my horizon? What is in my world that needs to be changed? How do I go about doing that?"

We see this by people purchasing all these books that are so popular these days and the various shows, even the popular media on television. This is part of finding ways of reaching out to each other in a different kind of way. This is the soul connection. This is the self-awareness, self-expression, shifting from ego to essence—who am I really and what am I really about here? What is this family unit that I am part of? What is it really about? When I see the things that are going on around me in the world that provoke consternation and fear in me, what is that about? How am I a part of this much bigger picture?

This is a search that people are really actively engaged in, and I think we're talking about some of the solutions to that. There are places for people to start to make connections and experience the awareness that "I'm not in this alone. I'm part of a much larger movement, a much larger sense of direction and I'm no longer a stranger in a strange land. I'm truly part of what some people would call the new majority."

Q: Yes. Lynne Twist talks about "awakening the dreamer." Carolyn, are we awakening?

Carolyn: Absolutely. I think the great search for the average American, the average person on the planet, is the search to know that whatever it is that we're doing in our lives, our soul longs to know that what we are doing is meaningful, whether it means raising a loving family or doing some big project out there in the world.

Is humanity awakening? Absolutely.

I'm very, very hopeful for humanity. Knowing the large numbers, the millions and millions—it might be even more than a billion people—who are all working in their own ways for positive change, and knowing that with technology we can connect with one another, I'm feeling very positive for and about our human family.

Barbara: I think we're being born as a universal humanity, and most images of global peace, of nonviolence and justice feel to me like corrections of a system, rather than the emergence of something we haven't seen before.

My own sense is that it's going to be an emergent species and I feel personally called to serve everyone anywhere who senses something emergent within themselves that hasn't yet been fully expressed. If it's truly emergent, then we have to be open to newness.

If I was a single cell dying in the seas of early Earth, could I have imagined photosynthesis in the biosphere? If you were the most intelligent animal, could you possibly have imagined Homo sapiens? If you were a human coming to the edge of individuality and materialism destroying your planet, could you really imagine a planetary universal culture born with the full capacity—spiritual, social and technological?

I, as an evolutionary soul, am keeping my mind open at the top because I find almost every vision of a peaceful, just world to be actually so limiting. If we did get there, we'd be immediately discontent.

Q: I love how you began by saying that peace is not a goal. It's something very different. I think a lot of us have set peace out there as the goal.

Barbara: All the things we're learning about nonviolence in communication are absolutely vital, but it's almost like a newborn baby. There are things that are immediately important so that the organism can function. Then there's the growth of that organism. You think of planet Earth as a living system in a solar system, in a universe as an evolutionary soul, an evolutionary spirituality. You don't limit God to fixing everything the way it is.

Q: *Let's take it down to the practical level. If we need to know what's the most urgent, what's the highest priority, what's the thing that must happen immediately to help this baby grow up? What would be a practical step?*

Carolyn: What I do in my daily life to support this change is to practice nonjudgment, nonattachment and nonresistance. I find that when I am able to do that, I am creating peace in my own little universe and I am contributing to the whole.

John: For me, it really starts with being quiet, listening to myself, by being surrounded by uplifting music, reading inspirational writings, and in the societal context, trying to be with people that are part of the field. In that way, I'm with people who are peaceful in their own being and who support and nurture that peace so that I can then fully express who I am in that context as well.

Barbara: I'd add to that something that's been my tradition, which is journal writing. I will frame a question in my journal, particularly if it's something that's disturbing me. I'll try to be clear about everything about it. Then I develop a poised mind and ask for what wants to be born out of the challenge that I might be facing.

It always is an evolutionary driver moving me towards a greater expression or potential. I think the purpose of life is expressing its full potential. When I'm posing a question, the process always releases the tension by revealing that it's an emergent quality inside myself pressing to get forward. That's my nature.

*****

Learn more about **Barbara Marx Hubbard** and the **Foundation for Conscious Evolution** at *www.barbaramarxhubbard.com.*

Information about Global Family with **Carolyn Anderson** and **John Zwerver** is online at *www.globalfamily.net*. Carolyn, John and Barbara also offer programs through their retreat center at Hummingbird Ranch, online at *www.hummingbirdlivingschool .org*.

*****

Reflection Points

John Zwerver commented that peace is our natural state. He says, "When we're not at peace, when we realize that we are in conflict or in some kind of confusion, then it's important to check back in and say, 'What's going on here?'" Notice where you see evidence of a lack of peace, in your life and in the world. In what ways are you aware of a disconnection with Source in these instances?

Barbara Marx Hubbard states, "You have to look at it with evolutionary eyes, and then you say not so much what went wrong, but 'What's going right?'" What do you see in your life and in the world that is going *right*?

The Peacebuilder Challenge

Begin keeping a "Peace Journal" to address issues or topics that may be disturbing you. Be clear about what the issue is, and why it is bothering you, then pose your mind to answer the question: "What wants to be born out of this challenge?" Capture your thoughts and insights in your journal as each issue arises.

3

A VIEW OF OUR PLANET

Edgar Mitchell

*Apollo 14 astronaut Edgar Mitchell is one of the few human beings
to glimpse our planet from the surface of the moon. During his 1971
flight, he experienced a profound sense of universal connectedness,
inspiring him to found the Institute of Noetic Sciences (IONS). I
talked with him about his unique "big picture" perspective on the
prospects for peace on Earth.*

"There is no certainty whatsoever that this civilization
and this planet has to survive. We must learn to get
along peacefully with each other, lest we unleash the
powerful, destructive technologies that we have
invented."
—Edgar Mitchell, Apollo 14 astronaut and founder
of the Institute of Noetic Sciences

Q: Ed, you are one of the few people who has had the privilege of walking on the moon. You've had an experience of seeing our planet as that beautiful blue ball hovering in space. How did your experience in space impact the way you see our world?

It's what I call the "big-picture effect." We start to see this planet and ourselves from a different perspective. Instead of being as big as it is, you get out there and it looks very small. Particularly when we go into the pictures from the Hubble telescope, we see how immense the observable universe is. It humbles you a great deal to realize just how small we are, and in a larger scheme of things, really pretty insignificant.

However, seeing the earth in that perspective makes you want to tell the world, "Hey, we've got to think in a different way!" One of the most important ways in which we can think is learning to get along better. We learn to get our act together, and to see ourselves as universal citizens as opposed to just local kids in some valley or some little town in the world.

Q: Yes, so there's so much happening in the world right now. Do you think we're at a pivot point?

We certainly, I believe, are at a tipping point. Here's what I say to young people when I'm speaking to them to help put it in perspective:

My great-grandparents came across from South Georgia to West Texas in covered wagons to start a new life shortly after our Civil War in the 1870s. Of course, railroads weren't complete across the south and the west. Automobiles hadn't been invented and electric lights hadn't been invented. My father was born shortly after the Wright brothers made the first flight at the beginning of the 20th century, and I went to the moon.

So we went from traveling by covered wagon to going to the moon by rocket in just under a century. That's pretty impressive. For thousands of years before that, we humans walked or rode elephants, horses, camels or whatever else we did for locomotion.

A few thousand years ago, the South Sea Islanders dug out canoes and started exploring the vast Pacific, and then the Phoenicians started exploring the Mediterranean. Therefore, your steps and those are only a few thousand years apart.

But in the last hundred years, all of this that we are now experiencing is essentially a runaway technology. In the very near past, a global economic system almost collapsed upon itself. So we have some things to think about.

Q: *Yes, we do. As you take that and project it forward, what do you see unraveling, unfolding or evolving from this?*

I think we can pull it off. We can get by it. I think if we put our minds to it, we can solve the climate problems that we have, the sustainability problems that have cropped up here.

If you look at every measure of human activity, it's on an exponential growth curve. And if you know a little bit of mathematics at all from high school, it should be obvious that the exponential route can't continue indefinitely in a finite space. This little planet is a finite space. So we are approaching a tipping point that we've been talking about for the last 30 or 40 years now, knowing it was coming.

For example, peak oil is a bonus. A few other measures of nonrenewable resources are near exhaustion, so we have to rethink for ourselves exactly what's going on here and what we can do about it. Our consumerism, our self-service and our greed have been our undoing, and we're going to have to look at that.

Q: What do you do mathematically if there is exponential growth and we do have a finite space? What needs to shift?

We have to learn service to the greater good, service to each other, and service to the whole. President Kennedy said at his inauguration, "Ask not what your country can do for you; ask what you can do for your country." We have to think on a global scale now. What can we do to keep our civilization from collapsing from our own greed, over-consumption, overpopulation, overuse of resources?

It begins with us right here inside. We have to start learning to be peaceful with each other and resolve our differences—sort of balancing conflict, but learning to think in the bigger picture of the finiteness of our planet and what we're doing to it.

Some say, think green. Okay, that's part of it. Think green and think sustainable. Ask how many new-and-improved bottles of detergent do you need a month? How many new-and-improved computers or whatever? How much do we need to consume to really make a satisfying life? It's gotten out of hand.

Q: Edgar, what does peace mean to you?

It means learning to work with people, to love nature, to love our civilization, to be respectful and caring of all people. We have to learn to get along with everybody because we're all in this together. It's a matter of learning to get along. It's a matter of learning to live more simply and get away from how much we can have, what material goods we can have, and learn to move toward a more spiritual life. What that means to me is service to the greater good as opposed to service to ego.

Q: You're the founder of the Institute of Noetic Sciences (IONS). The mission of IONS is to advance the science of consciousness and human experience, and to serve individual and collective transformation. I hear you talking about the individual transformation. What are some of your own personal practices for holding the consciousness of peace?

I have been a meditator for more than 40 years now, and meditation helps put one in the mindset to be connected with others.

Now we can bring the science to this. When you're connected with folks—your children, your lovers, your parents, your friends—there's a quantum resonance that begins to take place that we can now describe in science.

Since the discovery of the quantum world back in the beginning of the 20th century, the physics community has thought and said, "This really only pertains to subatomic matter. It really doesn't pertain to our scale size." It turns out that's just wrong. It pertains to everything.

One of the most important things of life is that emotional aspects come right from the quantum level. When we learn to use that to our benefit and for the benefit of the greater good, and learn to project the caring, the love and the understanding that comes with being a very conscious, open person, this transformation is made much easier, and that's what we're talking about. It's changing our thinking, changing our approach to life.

For the ancient Greeks, it was called *metanoia*—change of mind, change of heart. In Zen, there's the *satori*. In ancient Sanskrit, it's *samadhi*. In other words, in each culture going back for centuries, we have a language describing these transformational transcendent processes. They're the root of our religions.

But quite often, with our religions being political systems, they go ahead and go somewhere else. But it all begins with the transcendent experience.

Q: *Where does the collective transformation tie into this?*

It has to go from person to person. Add more people to it.

In other words, we're pretty good at consumerism. I mean once we develop the technology, we can produce all sorts of wonderful goods and products to keep us occupied and whet our appetites. This is why bringing the science of consciousness in is so important.

In the 400 years since science evolved, consciousness was not part of it, and that was because of René Descartes. Writing during the 17th century, he claimed that body and mind, physicality and spirituality, belong to two different realms of reality and never truly should meet. Science grew up as a materialist, reductionist concept.

It began 400 years ago, and it's only in the late 20th century that they even embrace quantum mechanics. Quantum physics showed at the beginning of the 20th century that the Cartesian concept was wrong. We haven't really started to apply it and utilize it until late in the 20th century.

That's what consciousness studies are all about. That's why IONS has been studying and helping to promote this full notion of transformation and transcendence on the personal, the group and the societal level.

Q: *I think that some of the most exciting work that's out there is this science of consciousness and there are so many interesting studies being done. What are some of the most recent findings or the most recent results you've seen through your work with IONS?*

It's all exciting. It's the fact that we find in nature the way nature, the world, the universe is put together. The real question I ask is "How does this transcendence take place?"

It happened to me on the flight back from the moon, and it's what I call a "big picture"—seeing Earth as just a small, small, little part of this immense universe we're in. It makes you very humble.

That was why I started IONS. It's to apply these types of ideas and principles to see what we could do with them; but since I'm a scientist by nature, I wanted to see what we could do in science to help validate this. And it's working.

Q: What is your vision for what we can create when we come together in this consciousness and set the intention for caring for our planet?

There is no certainty whatsoever that this civilization and this planet has to survive. In other words, since World War II or during the whole 20th century, we have created enormous technology, but we have been warlike. We have created the most powerful nuclear technologies that could, if unleashed, destroy the whole world.

So we must learn to get along peacefully with each other lest we unleash these powerful, destructive technologies that we have invented. That's the most important thing.

We will go to Mars. I've said this in my lectures quite frequently. We will go to Mars, of course. But when we go and look back at this tiny little planet, Earth will seem much, much smaller, like just a little star in the sky.

It would be kind of foolish to say, "I came from the United States, Canada, Israel, France, Germany," or wherever. No, we came from Earth and we don't have our act together to do that yet.

We've got to get our act together as a civilization if we're going to go into space; and we are going because, remember, our sun will burn out in another couple of billion years. Now that seems like a long time, but our sun is halfway through its lifecycle, and if we're going to survive as a civilization, we're going to have to get off this planet in due course. That means we've got to get our act together and operate as a civilization. First of all, we've got to survive because we're not on a sustainable path.

Q: For us as individuals who are loving the idea of being peace-builders in the world, what's the one thing you would recommend that we can do in our lives today to affect the collective consciousness?

You have to practice what I'm talking about. As individuals, believe in it. You have to believe in it with passion. We have the science to back up what we're talking about on our lack of sustainability, and at IONS, we're creating the science that shows that transcendence is a doable thing. We can do it. We just have to learn to practice it. So education is a part of it, then walking our talk is the next part of it.

*****

Edgar Mitchell is the founder of the Institute of Noetic Sciences (*www.noetic.org*), serving an emerging movement of globally conscious citizens dedicated to manifesting our highest capacities. He believes that consciousness is essential to a paradigm shift that will lead to a more sustainable world. You can learn more about Edgar Mitchell, including his articles and essays on world peace from the Universal Peace Conference, at *www.edmitchellapollo14.com.*

*****

Reflection Points:

Edgar Mitchell talked about thinking beyond what the world can do for you, and instead focusing on what you can do for the world. What actions, large or small, do you take consciously to demonstrate your care for life on our planet? What actions, large or small, could you begin taking to be a greater steward of our natural resources?

Edgar mentioned that for more than 400 years, science was based on a false notion that claimed that body and mind were two different realms of reality. How does our new understanding of quantum mechanics impact your understanding of what it means to be a "peacebuilder"? How do/could you integrate peace practices in mind, body and spirit?

The Peacebuilder Challenge:

Identify one action, large or small, that you will commit to doing in order to be a better steward of the natural resources of our planet. It could be as simple as bringing cloth bags to the grocery store (instead of using paper or plastic), unsubscribing from unwanted junk mail you receive, riding your bike for short errands, or many other inspired challenges. You can find more creative, green-living ideas at *www.care2.com/greenliving.*

4

THE NEW PEACE MOVEMENT

Stephen Dinan and Lawrence Ellis

Across the country, local grassroots initiatives like San Francisco's Summer of Peace project are bringing people together to create dialogues about how we can create a lasting, sustainable peace both from the inside out and from the outside in. I talked with two of the project's leaders, Stephen Dinan, founder and CEO of The Shift Network, and Lawrence Ellis, spiritual teacher, activist and complexity-science consultant.

> "Peace is not the absence of conflict; it is really the optimal synergy between all of our members of society, all sectors, as well as ourselves."
>
> —Stephen Dinan, Summer of Peace

Q: Lawrence, let's start by talking about Summer of Peace. What is the vision for this project?

Lawrence: Summer of Peace holds a vision of highlighting some of the best practices that can transform a culture of violence into a culture of peace in the Bay Area, from the individual level to the ecological level and everything in between.

We are not intending to lead all of the transformational efforts. Instead we highlight the best practitioners, luminaries, programs, et cetera, and bring them together in new ways for synergistic collaborations. We want to look at ways in which we can assist them in amplifying their works and proliferating them both in the Bay Area and beyond.

So we're about supporting the transformation of a culture that is steeped in conflict and violence, and moving towards this healthier culture. This includes events focused on arts and culture, on broad peacebuilding efforts, and on practical activities in neighborhoods—for example, peace potlucks that bring together local neighborhoods, or interventions in schools with groups like Challenge Day (*challengeday.org*).

Q: We became aware that there are literally dozens of great groups doing peacebuilding work in different sectors of society. However, there has not been a vision for them to come together to offer their work collaboratively and synergistically. When we all work together, the results are much more powerful.

If we look at it from a real bird's eye view, Stephen, what would you say peace means to you?

Stephen: Peace has had a connotation of being a little bit boring and passive. Not sexy or hip. So I think that part of what we really need to do in Summer of Peace is to rebrand peace as something that is sexy, that is hip, that is creative, that is dynamic, that is engaging.

Peace is not the absence of conflict; it is really the optimal synergy between all of our members of society, all sectors, as well as ourselves. When we are at peace with ourselves, we are not doing battle with any part of ourselves, which includes shadowy elements or self-destructive elements.

We have used Barbara Marx Hubbard's mapping of 12 sectors around a wheel of co-creation as a way to map how the different sectors of society can work together more effectively. There is something about this feeling where everybody has a seat at the table that creates harmonious creativity. Peace is a broader tent than just dealing with violence reduction. It is really about a new kind of society on the outside, and really having that sense of wholeness and oneness internally.

Lawrence: One distinct contribution that we are making with Summer of Peace is not only talking about what peace looks like, but also about how to manifest it using our fourfold framework for transformation: *inside-out, outside-in, top-down, bottom-up.*

Top-down strategies leverage legislative, judicial and other mandated forms of change. *Bottom-up* strategies focus on grassroots, community-based change. *Inside-out* involves "inner" transformational practices. *Outside-in* strategies leverage social media and web technologies to broadcast and amplify messages, and to build connections and enduring networks.

For me, peace means, in part, leveraging all of those approaches to get to this tripartite state we are talking about: the absence of overt conflict, plus individual mindfulness presence, plus this range of synergistic relationships.

Q: What would you say the essential foundations for peace would be?

Stephen: On the personal level you do need to have disciplines to deal with conflict internally and externally. You cannot have a peaceful society that does not begin with individual peace. There is a foundation of practice that supports that.

But I think that we also need to look at the social or community level, because that has a big impact on the individual. We need to have social communities that are based upon not using conflict, not using violence to settle conflicts, and that are promoting a collaborative, loving whole.

On a more macro level, we need to have government structures that allow participation and opportunity for the widest range of folks to be involved.

Violence is a last resort that people will turn to if they do not feel they have any other mechanism to deal with a situation. We need to have programs to build in these practices so that we have the inner tools to deal with conflict and violence, and so that our society really shifts to being as inclusive as possible, and has ways to resolve conflict between sectors.

Q: Lawrence, what do you think the missing piece is then, so far, in the approach to peacebuilding?

Lawrence: People often fail to realize that peace entails more than just the absence of overt violent conflict. Johan Galtung, the renowned "parent of peace studies," made the distinction between the absence of overt violent conflict, "negative peace," and the presence of collaborative, supportive, positive relationships, or "positive peace."

Many people define peace as "negative peace" only, and feel helpless to bring an end to the overt violence endemic to our society. So they give up on peacebuilding, thinking, There's nothing that a single individual like me can do to make a real dent in the violence in the world. We're just "apes who kill," and that's how it is and how it will always be.

So resignation sets in, and people give up their sense of agency. If they reframe peace in broader terms, to include "positive peace," then they realize that there are always things they can be doing to support peacebuilding. So that's one important distinction. That's a missing piece.

Our fourfold framework presents a model for people to become change-agents in multiple ways. Again, people often think of change only in "top down" ways: laws, policies, treaties, and so on. They think, I'm not a UN peacekeeper or any other role with power and influence. What can I do to make a difference?

When we highlight myriad practices and tools in the bottom-up, inside-out and outside-in dimensions, and showcase the positive effects of these tools and practices, people get jazzed! They learn how working in these dimensions often presents high-leverage ways to influence top-down changes.

Q: Stephen, how do we create a peace infrastructure that stretches from local to global?

Stephen: First of all, I think it is more about interconnecting pieces that are already there rather than having to create everything from scratch. There are a number of converging movements that are really trying to build this infrastructure. The most important on the national level that I see is the Department of Peace legislation and movement behind it (more info at *www.thepeacealliance.org*). This would be a cabinet level position that would be funded at a reasonable level focused on peacebuilding work.

And not just focused on an international level, but really focused on everything from domestic violence to recidivism rates to violence with teens. So it would become a national legislative priority and a line item in the budget too that would be right on the dashboard for the president.

If we are primarily orienting our money and legislation towards defense, which is one legitimate part of protecting our country against harm from the outside, we do not psychologically promote the culture of peace. We need to promote the culture of peace not just in our own country, but in the way we engage the rest of the world.

There is another interesting initiative called a National Peace Academy (*www.nationalpeaceacademy.us*) that trains the peace workers of tomorrow. Various people are working from different directions to create a more integrated peace infrastructure, which I think is going to help to amplify what is there and working.

Q: It is exciting to see people coming together on a local level, and I think we are seeing it across the country with initiatives like this. Lawrence, what are some of the most promising new programs that you have seen?

Lawrence: There are really so many. I will just highlight a few. Numerous organizations support taking a stand, commitment or vow to *be peace*—to practice peace consistently in thought, word and deed toward oneself, other humans, and all forms of life on Earth.

This does have to be a solid commitment to nonviolent ways of being, but it doesn't have to be "heavy." Hold it as practice: "Okay, I fell off the balance beam of being peace, of nonviolence in thought, word and deed. Now it's time to dust myself off and get back on the beam."

What's great is that anyone can take a stand, or make a vow, and use it as an anchor for peacebuilding practice all of their waking moments.

Recently, in schools ranging from elementary to university, there have been national and international headlines about the horrendous effects of bullying—from physical confrontations to cyber-bullying. Challenge Day is one of several excellent anti-bullying initiatives (*www.challengeday.org*).

Dan Savage's *It Gets Better* project (*www.itgetsbetter.org*) is an excellent resource for transforming violence against lesbian, gay, bisexual and transgender (LGBT) young people, who face rates of violence and suicide alarmingly above their heterosexual counterparts.

Generation Five (*www.generationfive.org*) aims to end child sex abuse within five generations. This may seem like an unattainable goal to some. However, the group's founder was emboldened by the precedents of other movements like the slavery abolition and women's suffrage movements. Change on such a massive scale is possible within five generations. Given that one in three girls and one in six boys is sexually abused before the age of 18, this is a small but key program making a difference.

I advocate doing anything and everything we can do to support the United Nations Convention on the Elimination of all forms of Discrimination Against Women (CEDAW) (*www.un.org/womenwatch/daw/cedaw*). Women and girls disproportionately suffer from numerous forms violence, and CEDAW is one approach for addressing this. Note that the United States has not yet ratified the convention, and there are many local actions we can take, which include getting our local municipalities to adopt CEDAW (*www.cedaw2011.org*).

Notably, many ancient wisdom traditions bring resources that have been tested and refined over millennia—and are just the medicine needed for these times. Some key frameworks for insight, and practices for transformation, can be found in the works of the International Council of Thirteen Indigenous Grandmothers (*www.grandmotherscouncil.org*), Angeles Arrien (*www.angelesarrien.com*), Malidoma Somé (*www.malidoma.com*), Sobonfu Somé (*www.sobonfu.com*) and other wisdom-keepers from Indigenous cultures.

Q: Stephen, let's talk more about the organizing framework for Summer of Peace—the top-down, bottom-up, inside-out, outside-in approach. We hear a lot about the concept of inside-out, so that might be a good place to start. What are some ways that you, personally, cultivate inner peace and harmony in your life on a daily basis?

Stephen: First of all I want to say we borrowed a lot of that framework from Van Jones, who I think is fantastic. He often said that change happens top-down, bottom-up and inside-out, and I just added the outside-in to include the media and social networking component.

We hosted a fundraiser here for *Art in Actio*n (*www .artinactionworld.org*). This group takes kids who have been oftentimes gang members, drug dealers, pretty rough-and-tumble adolescents and they help them create media. There are leadership skills taught, and they are creating a green-use media center. They are basically giving them job opportunities, and opportunities to create, innovate and gain leadership skills. So it is a kind of full-spectrum solution, which combines the four different quadrants we are talking about here.

For me, I try to meditate every morning. Also, yoga has really been helpful, because I find that pent-up tension in the body often leads to a little more aggression or feelings of frustration. To the extent that I can release bodily tension, I become a lot more peaceful as well. I would say that my relationship, in general, with my wife has been a really great practice ground of learning to live joyously and peacefully with each other.

Lawrence: We live in systems embedded in systems embedded in yet more systems, all deeply interconnected. One might be part of a dysfunctional—or even violent—social system, like a family. Maintaining an atmosphere of peace in such situations, like through a meditation practice, can help everyone.

We've probably all been in situations where a calm presence has helped to calm us. However, this alone may not shift the underlying root causes of the problem. It may be necessary, but often is not sufficient. Perhaps if I look more deeply, I see that the parents are physically abusive because they were abused as children—and that's all they learned. We can then take action at that level to transform the cycles of violence, perhaps through counseling, teaching parenting skills, and the like.

Perhaps there is stress because of economic structural violence—working members of the family are being stripped of their rights, and don't have the skills and tools to transform their despair and rage, and are exploding at home. We can then take action at the level of teaching inside-out tools to transform, while also supporting bottom-up grassroots campaigns for justice, designed to transform unjust top-down policies.

Practices that cultivate this deep sense of interdependence and interconnectedness are very key to me. I have drawn a lot on ancient traditions. I am a Buddhist teacher. I teach periodically at Spirit Rock Meditation Center, at the East Bay Meditation Center in Oakland, and other places. So meditation practice is very important to me, and I meditate daily.

Often my meditation practice is intertwined with my activist-in-the-world practices. Sometimes there's wisdom in

"Don't just sit there, do something!" I need to take action out in the world, and not just go about my daily business, or not just sit on my meditation cushion.

Sometimes there's wisdom in "Don't just do something, sit there!" Rather than acting in reactive mode, or from clouded vision, it's best to bring the suffering of the world to my meditation cushion. From that place of transformation-that-leads-to-calm-and-insight, deeper solutions often arise. Then, set with these, I can take wise, nonreactive action in the world.

I am also of African (a mix of Southern and Western African peoples), African-American and Tsalagi/Cherokee ancestry. My Indigenous—in particular, ancestral—practices for cultivating interconnectedness for deeply honoring our relatedness with other humans, with other species and with the Earth are critical.

Q: Talk about the "outside-in" approach. How can an individual use this outside-in approach to create peace in their home, in their communities and in the world?

Lawrence: One thing is critical: "Peace begins with me." Absolutely. We need to look at this not just in our relationship with everything else, but with these patterns of relating between *individual wholeness* or *coherence, group coherence* and *ecological coherence.*

For example, I can practice my meditation of letting peace begin with me, and if I put myself in a certain social setting where there is more coherence, it will literally change my neural pathways. We know that if you put a person in a certain family dynamic, for example, it affects the structure of their brain and the individual can bring peace to the group, but the group can also bring peace to the individual.

What happens to my nervous system, in terms of peaceful-ness, when I walk or spend hours in a redwood forest is differ-ent than what happens when I am in, to quote Bob Marley, "the concrete jungle." I have to practice in a different way to remain peaceful in that setting.

"Let peace begin with me" does not mean isolating our-selves; it means often putting ourselves in different contexts, conditions and circumstances—often in group settings, rather than kowtowing to the isolation which is so much the default in much of American society.

We are deeply interconnected. "Peace beginning with me" is also an outside-in job. We may "let peace begin with me," but be supported by a network of individuals, or a community of practice—a "beloved community" ideally.

My invitation, which may lead to the most dramatic peace, is to go deeply into the heart of that interconnection—with all of its chaos and all of its despair—and find one's solidity and grounding there, held in loving support by others, and holding them in loving support.

Stephen: We are social animals and we tend to look to the environment around us for signals as to what right behavior is. When we have communities or media that reflect back a more peaceful, creative, collaborative mode of living, then we are much more likely to do that ourselves. We sort of mirror that neurologically, in our biology and other things.

So, to the extent that we can create these positive social rein-forcements, cultural reinforcements, media reinforcements, we are acting as spreaders of peace. I think that individuals can do a lot more than they might imagine, especially with today's social media. You think of something like the gratitude dance, where this guy went around the world and did this little funny jig in front of all sorts of different cultures, and invited different people to join in, and it became a YouTube phenomenon (*www.wherethehellismatt.com*) and millions of people have seen these things. It becomes a sort of grassroots phenomena.

People can create their own little forms of media that they can post to reach out. They can create spiritual communities that reach into different neighborhoods where a culture of violence might be the operating principle. All of those things are relatively easy for us to do. We each do not just "be peace"; we broadcast peace or create peace environments for other people.

Q: *So, Lawrence, talk about Summer of Peace and how you are using that bottom-up, top-down approach.*

Lawrence: Bottom-up approaches focus on grassroots, community-based change. Again, a key function of Summer of Peace is to showcase and amplify great initiatives already under way. So we partner with a number of organizations.

One strategic partner, Urban Peace Movement (*urbanpeacemovement.org*), does great work on shifting the violent underpinnings of some aspects of youth and young-adult culture. They lead or sponsor a number of grassroots campaigns. Their *Silence the Violence* campaign has partnered with the mayor, city council members, the Oakland Raiders football team management, and other top-down legislative, elite celebrities, and other movers-and-shakers. So they have influence at top-down levels, and the success of their programs is probably playing a role shaping policies and laws.

We also use top-down entry point for change. We have a number of contacts in lots of local, city and other regional forms of government. We've met with city council representatives, mayors, congresspeople ... and we even have significant connections with the White House.

Clearly an example on a massive scale of the fourfold approach to change is occurring with the uprisings in North Africa, the Arabian Peninsula and Southwest Asia. Outside-in technologies like Facebook and Twitter have played a pivotal role in accelerating and enabling connections and networks that augment bottom-up social change. The bottom-up movement is aimed at transforming repressive top-down economic, political and related structures and systems. Finally, throughout the uprisings, the people have sustained themselves with prayer, visual and performing arts, music and dance, and the like.

Q: Stephen, what message of peace would you want to pass on to future generations?

Stephen: That is a big question. I would say that it is really time that we outgrow violence as an operating principle. We can move beyond war as the natural state of being between different countries.

I fundamentally believe that ours is the generation [for peace] and this is the time. Violence really is going to become something that is rare within our lifetimes, I believe, rather than the norm.

In order for us to make that transition from a baseline culture of violence to a baseline culture of peace globally does not mean we are going to eliminate all of it. But I think that the expectation will be that it really is no longer permissible for nations to be at war with each other, or for the kind of large-scale violence we have seen.

Lawrence: We live in a time of great peril. The ecological crisis alone threatens to destroy all life on the planet Earth—at least radically alter life from how we have known it. Seven out of 10 biologists believe we are in the midst of the fifth or sixth mass extinction. We do not know what that will do. It is mainly plant species, but in time the whole food chain could collapse.

My hope and my prayer is that the acts that we have done and that we are doing today—those of us who are walking mindfully on the planet as best as we can—will have brought about a shift in our global culture away from so much violence, and towards life-sustaining civilization. One of my key aspirations is that we return to what many of our ancestors knew: that we are all radically interconnected, that we need to walk gently on the Earth, honoring the Earth and honoring each other.

It is my hope and deep prayer and dream that we will have made it through this time of great unraveling, as it is often called, with systems in collapse—economic, psychological, political and the like. To one or two generations down the pike, I say, "Cultivate clear perspectives and insights, develop collaborative and loving connections, and take right action. Do the right thing—even and especially when it feels hopeless or overwhelming, because that is when it is most needed."

Gandhi said, "Whatever you do is insignificant, but it is very important that you do it." I think that he meant "insignificant" not in consequence but in scale. That is, our actions may seem small, but each one contributes a vital component to the web of life. For the web to be whole, we must each play our part.

Q: Lawrence, do you believe that peace is a realistic goal?

Lawrence: I do believe peace is a realistic goal. Great luminaries from across the millennia, on all continents, have shown us that we can maintain "positive peace" in extremely challenging external circumstances. What they did was not just for them, leaving it unavailable to us mere mortals. It was for us too. "Positive peace" is a practice. If you learn about the lives of Aung San Suu Kyi, Martin Luther King Jr., Mohandas Gandhi, Mother Teresa, Rigoberta Menchu, Wangari Maathai and others, you learn that they have or had foibles, flaws and failures. They are or were profoundly human.

"Positive peace" was a practice for them—and it is for us too. We may get agitated, or fall into forgetfulness, or tumble into despair. Then we notice. We reawaken. We begin practicing anew. We move towards mastery with practice—thought by thought, word by word, action by action.

As for the absence of conflagrations, we can debate academically. However, independent of whether we, as a species, ever achieve a state of no war, we can all head in that direction. It's like the North Star. We may never get there, but we head in the direction of less violence, of more peace. It's about having the courage, fortitude, vision and mindfulness to take right action, to come from a place of being peace, no matter what the outcomes. It's about letting it begin with me—beginning after beginning after beginning.

*****

Stephen Dinan is the creator of the Shift in Action program of the Institute of Noetic Sciences, serving 10,000 global members (*www.noetic.org*). Stephen is the co-founder and chair of the board of Summer of Peace (*www.summerofpeace.net*).

Lawrence Ellis (*www.LawrenceEllis.org* and *www.Pathsto Change.net*) is a complexity science organizational consultant (one who applies insights from the study of complex systems in nature, society and science to human organizations), a spiritual teacher and an activist. He studied the application of Gandhian nonviolence to individual and large-scale change on a Rhodes Scholarship at Oxford University. He was the interim executive director of Summer of Peace (*www.summerofpeace.net*).

*****

Reflection Points

What are some ways that you cultivate peace from the "inside-out"? How often do you use these practices in times of conflict or challenge?

How supportive is your environment (work, home, neighborhood, and so on) for supporting you in maintaining a peace-filled presence?

The Peacebuilder Challenge

Research nonprofit programs in your community that are building an infrastructure of peace. (For example, youth programs, arts/culture, civic organizations, political alliances, et cetera) Attend one of their meetings or fundraisers to learn more about their goals and needs. Visit *www.yourcause.com* to spark some ideas!

5

SERVICE AND MINDFULNESS

His Holiness Karma Kuchen Rinpoche

From his first official tour of America, His Holiness Karma Kuchen Rinpoche, the 12th throne holder of the Palyul Lineage of Tibetan Buddhism, joined me for an online radio conversation. Speaking through his translator, he shared an international, interfaith perspective on the path to peace and how to shift our mindset in a way that fosters love and compassion.

> "I contemplate my motivation—am I motivated with an intention to benefit others, or motivated with an intention to harm others? By contemplating like that, I identify the action that would bring benefits to others. Then I try to do that."
>
> —His Holiness, Karma Kuchen Rinpoche,
> the Palyul Lineage

Q: Thank you for being here with us. We welcome you to America. What is the purpose of your visit?

Rinpoche: The main purpose is taking this tour. There are many people that I know and many others that are interested in creating this connection. I want to give an opportunity to connect with anyone who is willing to practice Buddhism or the spiritual path.

Q: We are very honored to have you here with us. Is there anything that you've experienced in terms of the people that you've met or the culture that has surprised you?

The surprising thing is that there are many people, non-Buddhists, who show interest in Buddhism. That was a surprise for me.

Q: What does peace mean to you?

Peace is not only concerned with one or two people, but it applies to all people living on this planet who are concerned and working together to help each other. So that's one thing. Not only taking care of human beings, but also taking care of all the external environments. Peace happens through the people and through the environment. This is what I see as peace.

Q: As an individual wanting to support peace on our planet, where do we begin? What can we do?

We start as an individual, then as a whole. I contemplate my motivation—is it motivated with an intention to benefit others, or is it motivated with an intention to harm others? By contemplating like this, I identify the action I think would bring benefits to others. Then I try to do that.

If that action is being motivated with an evil intent, I try to reduce that as much as possible. This is how one individual can help others and help in developing peace.

Q: What do you believe is the cause of disharmony within the individual?

The disharmony is basically concerned with discontent. We have some kind of goal and we want to accomplish that, but then there are conditions which hinder the accomplishing of that goal. Then people get discontent. This is where the disharmony starts.

Q: How does that show up when people get into conflict with each other? What is the source of conflict?

That conflict is just the discontentment. It's just because we, as individuals, have all these different kinds of emotions and thoughts. Discontentment is the root of all this conflict.

Q: If we were to look at this from the perspective of nations, how do we resolve conflicts as a nation?

To resolve conflict between different nations, what we have to do as a nation, first, is follow wise advice. We must also think about human rights, humanitarian thoughts and have that civic sense. We must have a way, like a constitution or law, that provides stability in the government for each particular nation. So that is most important: each nation having a constitution and laws that are very firm and stable.

Q: Here in our Western world, what message would you want to share with the American people about how we can contribute to peace on the planet?

Generally, what we have now is that we are so self-centered, just thinking about fulfilling our self-interest. We must give up that self-interest and self attitude, and think about benefitting others. To have that calm and very kindhearted mind is important, because how we experience things depends upon one's own mind.

With that kindhearted mind, the next step is not to belittle or discriminate against those people who are less fortunate than us. We must show them compassion, love and kindness. Then those people who are less fortunate see that others can respect and honor them. Honor their interest. Likewise, having that mutual understanding is important. Mutual understanding— which comes from love and kindness—is the key to the peace. This is what I would request everyone to cultivate.

Q: What spiritual practices can we implement that will best help us to do that, to be less self-centered?

We have to think about other beings, try to help other sentient beings and have concern about others. That's the mind-training. It's not just thinking about one or two individuals. We are sentient beings and all sentient beings need love and compassion.

Developing that uncontrived, unconditional compassion towards all sentient beings requires mind-training again and again. Gradually, it brings genuine compassion towards all sentient beings. If we're able to develop that genuine compassion, that would be the way to reduce our self-centeredness.

Q: Rinpoche, what role do you think religion plays in supporting peace on the planet?

Peace first requires a strong government, or the foundation which makes the country stable. We then have to share the message that basically all religions are teaching us peace. We must take this message of peace and try to teach people, print books and booklets, and create the media so that this message can be given to all people. Make them understand that this is the real message of religion.

Q: From the Buddhist tradition, what do you teach is the inner path to peace?

In Buddhism, to tame our mind is important. We tame our mind because if we are not able to tame our own mind, then it would be difficult to benefit others. We then try to reduce what we call the three afflicted emotions: having less desire, less anger, and less ignorance. We try to reduce all those emotions.

Try to tame the mind and gain mastery over the mind. Then in that way, there will be less emotions and more truth. Taming our mind is how we can develop inner peace.

Q: Why is it so challenging for so many of us to tame our minds?

The main thing is that we do not have trust and confidence in the path.

Q: As we look around the planet and here in the United States, people everywhere, it seems, are being impacted by shifts in the global economy, shifts in the environment as you were mentioning. Some people might say we have a long way to go before we reach a reality that might be described as peaceful. Do you think that we're closer to peace than we were a generation ago?

We are getting close to peace, but the problem is that people are so busy with their own work. They like to keep themselves busy. But I do believe that we're getting closer to peace.

Q: What do you think it will take to motivate people to step outside of their busyness to help create that peaceful world?

In this time where people are so very busy, we must still find the time to think about all the Buddhas or whatever they believe in. It is particularly important in these times when it is so busy.

In all religions, it is important to remember your deities. Then your blessing can be more powerful and you can more easily receive that blessing.

If you remember your gods, the deities or Buddha, then you will remember whatever path you are following. That would be the solution.

Q: What is your vision for what we can create as humanity as we step into this awareness that you're describing?

Speaking in relation with the Buddha Dharma, if we abandon our self-centeredness and try to benefit other beings, everything will turn into positive outcomes.

*****

His Holiness Karma Kuchen Rinpoche is the 12th throne holder of the Palyul Lineage of Tibetan Buddhism (*www.palyul.org*). The significant achievement of Karma Kuchen Rinpoche since his arrival in Tibet was that he had built many temples, stupas, prayer wheels, images of deities and other objects of veneration and faith. Under the direction of His Holiness Penor Rinpoche, he built a grand and magnificent temple within the monastery premises.

*****

Reflection Points

Rinpoche teaches that disharmony starts with discontent. In what areas of your life are you feeling discontent? How could you shift your mindset to support you in cultivating thoughts that bring you a greater sense of peace?

In the midst of the busyness of your day, how do you remind yourself to stay centered in your faith?

The Peacebuilder Challenge

Visit a spiritual center or religious organization outside your usual spiritual affiliations. Or visit with a friend or colleague whose religious background is different from your own. Ask questions and seek to find where your ideologies have common ground. Notice and appreciate the differences without judgment or attachment.

6

IT'S HOW WE VIEW EACH OTHER

Dr. John Demartini

Many of us know Dr. John Demartini from the hit movie The
Secret. *He is also a best-selling author and spiritual teacher who
travels extensively, bringing wisdom and insights to people all over
the world. His unique teachings about values assessment revolve
around a quintessential understanding of Oneness. He joins us to
share his method for seeing through the eyes of inner peace.*

> "I've been probing into the mysteries of life and the
> cosmological and astrophysical principles for 39 years.
> Anytime I don't see a Hidden Order, I feel it's my
> responsibility to look again."
>   —Dr. John Demartini, the Demartini Institute

*Q: Dr. Demartini, what have you found out about the correlation
between the inner mindset and our outer experience or our manifestations?*

I believe that our innermost dominant thoughts truly do
impact our outermost tangible realities. Our sensory and motor
sides, our attention and intention are both reflections of each

other. If we see a world outside that we're stressed by, then it indicates an inner stressing going on. We're projecting it because when we see the outer order, we have the inner order and vice versa. These worlds are reciprocal reflections.

Q: Tell us how this applies to creating and manifesting the vision of a more peaceful world.

First, I believe that every individual lives according to a set of priorities, a set of values. When we meet people, if we project our values onto them, expect them to live according to our values, and care less about them than our own values, we'll project ourselves onto them, and they won't appreciate that. There will be resistance. If we minimize ourselves, we end up sacrificing our values for theirs and that doesn't work either.

But if we care enough to see that they are reflections of us, and if we care enough to communicate what's important to us in terms of what's important to them in their values, now we end up in a dialogue instead of an alternating monologue. We now have, you might say, a peaceful relationship. We now realize that the seer, the seeing and the seen are the same, and they're equal. We have harmony.

That's the secret of relationship dynamics, whether it be individuals, collective or global.

Q: That's really the heart of peace. What does peace mean to you?

I would say what Schopenhauer said: We become ourselves to the degree that we make everyone else ourselves. When we realize that whatever we see in others is a part of us. Any part of us that we deny, they are bringing to our awareness. If we can own that and find out how it serves us, we can embrace it within ourselves and appreciate them for bringing it to our awareness and helping us love another part of ourselves.

When we do, we have an inner poise, an inner presence, an inner purpose, an inner power and an inner patience which we call peace.

Q: Your book is called From Stress to Success in Just 31 Days. *How does stress impact the journey to inner peace?*

We have a set of values or a set of priorities that we live by. Anytime we set goals and objectives that are congruent and aligned with our highest values, we are basically living true to ourselves. We have an inner peace because we're now poised and present with ourselves.

But at any time we subordinate to outer influences and try to be somebody we're not, or try to project onto others things which they are not, we run into snags. Now we're fighting within ourselves and trying to be somebody we're not, or trying to get other people to be somebody they're not, and there's a natural resistance in that.

Everybody wants to be loved and appreciated for who they are. It's important for us to be true and authentic with our own goals and objectives. To the degree that we have congruency, we have an inner calmness, an inner peace.

When we honor other people for their values, and don't expect anything but for them to live according to their values, then there's a congruency between them and within them. That's what allows a harmonious dynamic to occur on any level from individual to global.

As you look around the world with a global perspective, it's easy to see things to stress out about. We could look at global warming, poverty, war or violence. If you're looking for it, you can find something to be stressful about.

But I really believe in a Higher Order. I've been probing into the mysteries of life and the cosmological and astrophysical principles for 39 years. Anytime I don't see a Hidden Order, I feel it's my responsibility to look again.

I believe that there is truly a Divine Intelligence and Divine Order and Presence there at all times. If I don't see it, my job is to go and ask a new set of questions until it's revealed to me. When I do, I'm in a state of gratitude for the Presence, and instead of me proposing my artificial values unto things, I am then able to communicate what's important to me in terms of a Hidden Order.

I believe that if I see an event that I think is terrible and out of order, my job is to go and find out, "What is the higher purpose of this? Is it basically an expression of people's repressions? Are people projecting unrealistic expectations?"

I try to find out what it is. Instead of just being upset about it, I try to find a solution to that. I find there's a Hidden Order and it's there ultimately to teach us on an individual or a collective basis how to love and appreciate ourselves and others in the journey.

Q: *In the midst of that, do you ever sense a feeling of urgency around what you see?*

My feeling of urgency is based on how and to what degree I don't see the order in it. When I see the order in it, I'm just grateful. When you love people for who they are, they turn into who you love. Instead of me jumping in and trying to fix somebody because of my misinterpretation, I'd rather go back, look at my interpretation, find the Hidden Order and appreciate them for their role.

When I look on a global level, I do the same. Instead of reacting, I often say, "It's wiser to go back, reflect and then act before I react." A lot of times, I think I'm fixing something, but it's usually because of my misinterpretation.

People don't want to be fixed. They want to be loved. Once I find out what their set of values are, and then expect their actions to be according to their values (and not mine), I find a Hidden Order in them and I'm appreciative of what they're doing. I now love them for who they are and they turn into who I love by doing so.

Q: One thing I've observed is that when there's a sense of urgency, people leap into action. When the urgency is gone, the issue tends to disappear on the horizon. So without that sense of urgency, what then becomes the impetus for forward motion?

I've had events in my life that I initially thought were terrible, tragic, traumatizing or whatever. Then a day, a week, a month, a year or five years later, I'd look back and say, "Thank God that occurred." I didn't see how it was serving me initially. In truth, it has served me in immense ways and I wouldn't want it any other way.

Instead of me having the wisdom of the ages through the aging process, I'd rather go and awaken my mind intuitively to questions that allow me to see the magnificence and the hidden benefits of it now. I'd rather have the wisdom of the ages without the aging process, in other words.

What I do now is I stop. Instead of first initially interpreting something as devastating, I go in and ask, "What could be the benefits of this? How could the Divine Plan be working at this moment?" When I do that instead of fixing it, or trying to quickly fix and react to it, I find a Hidden Order. I find that there's a nonlocally entangled quantum phenomenon that occurs—a complementation of opposites.

When we love things, there's a shift that occurs. Now we have the power to transform it instead of react to it. I have found that this, in the long run, is a greater, more powerful way of getting things accomplished. Instead of reacting, I find it's wiser to act.

Now the urgency is to find the order in it and then thank the person, because you get farther by doing that than you ever do by trying to fix the person.

I think having gratitude for a Higher Order allows me to do more in life because every time I've thought, That person is off-base. They are wrong. They're not matching my reality and they're not matching what I think is peace in the world, I usually run into resistance, and now I'm at war inside myself over the thing that I think needs fixing. I'm trying to solve the war, but I'm creating the war in the process.

Q: When you look at the world through that lens of peace, what do you see that you're grateful for?

Albert Einstein was awed and humbled by the Intelligence that permeates the universe. He constructed a concept of God according to the natural laws. But when he probed into it, he said, "The more I probe into it, the more humble I get behind what's actually occurring."

Heraclitus said 2,480 years ago that there was a dynamic equilibrium of complementary opposites, and when man awakens to see this, he is appreciative, sees it and then doesn't have to fix it. He is appreciative of it and when he loves it, he changes it dynamically.

I'd rather come from the global perspective and appreciate other people's values and honor them. I get more done that way.

*****

Dr. John Demartini (*www.drdemartini.com*) is considered one of the world's leading authorities on human behavior and personal development. He is the founder of the Demartini Institute, a private research and education organization with a curriculum of more than 72 different courses covering multiple aspects of human development. He has worked in partnership with educational organizations in South Africa in an effort to empower and inspire young adults from disadvantaged backgrounds.

*****

Reflection Points:

Dr. Demartini states, "If we see a world outside that we're stressed by, then it indicates an inner stressing going on." What are the things you see in the world that cause you the most stress? In what ways do you notice a correlation between the outer and inner worlds?

Are there any areas of conflict in your life that you believe require urgent action? How can you use this idea of "action versus reaction" to find peace in this situation?

The Peacebuilder Challenge:

Determine your core values. You may want to use a process like Dr. Demartini's free values hierarchy assessment online at *http://drdemartini.com/value_determination.*

7

THE VIRUS OF COMPETITION

B.J. Dohrmann

B.J. Dohrmann sets the bar for collaboration and cooperation in the world of business. His program has helped entrepreneurs, business owners and corporate executives step into a new economic paradigm based on unifying principles rather than competitive advantage. He is the chairman of CEO Space. He has provided conferences for more than 65,000 business leaders interested in experiencing accelerated business growth and prosperity.

> "If we cooperate, we can have the most exciting explo-
> ration that's ever happened in the history of con-
> sciousness. And if we don't cooperate, we'll use our
> weapons and the planet will start again."
> —B.J. Dohrmann, chairman of CEO Space

Q: Berny, tell us a little bit about your philosophy on collaboration versus competition.

The mother of all viruses on the human mind today is the virus of *competition* and the way we think when we organize ourselves in fear, punishment and exploitation. It has been a wrong model.

In the world of government and business, we get so much less out of performance. We see the environmental meltdown. We can do all the things we need to do if we begin to collaborate, cooperate and organize ourselves so that diversity is honored.

It doesn't matter whether we are Hindu or Buddhist, GED or Ph.D., what our skin color and background is, whether we're Sunni, Wahhabi or Shiite. We celebrate your music, your song, your dress, your dance. We celebrate how interesting it is, and we remove this whole thought of competition. It's a terrible drain on the future and it leads us to fire our weapons. We are doomed if we continue down that path.

Cooperative thinking is the future. We've been 20-plus years working in public education and putting out college-level curriculums that build organizational theory on the practice of cooperation versus competition. It is the way to world peace and it is the only way. We have to start there. In other words, there has to be a single source line or code to reprogram what is going on in our brains: the illusion that competition has anything good to offer us.

Q: You talk about our gifts and our passions. Growing up, I remember all the things that I loved to do: speaking, art, dancing, et cetera. In every discipline, there was always a competition or an evaluation. We're always competing. It's a mindset. What gave the old mindset so much strength and power to begin with?

It's part of our evolution. We started with a tribal, much more cooperative society. We learned to plant seeds and ended up by rivers. Then we started a feudal kind of society that is very competitive because if you had a bigger garden, we'd try to take it over. This happened for 8,000 years. Then we have the industrial revolution which made a guy on the streets as wealthy as a baron in 24 months, so they needed a new model and we had *competitive capitalism* emerge from *competitive feudalism*. Karl Marx tried to fix that with communism, but he created *competitive bureaucracy,* which was worse than *competitive capitalism.*

The solution is actually just identifying the source problem and organizing ourselves with systems, accountability, full transparency and reportability. All the greed goes away because cooperation doesn't have any secrets. Competition has secrets. Cooperation does not. Everybody is trying to make a better planet and everybody helps everybody else. There is accountability in the cooperation system.

I'm going to be at the United Nations next week with the president of the General Assembly and Ambassador Byron Blake, probably one of the greatest peacemakers in the world. We're taking the old competitive capitalism, and declaring it is a failed model. Its systems can never be repaired. If we try to repair it, we will just get more meltdowns in the future. Our children will pay the price for generations.

We need to get the whole world on a cooperative capitalism model—and it is coming. Governments are looking at real solutions. They can see the drain, they just can't keep up. They see the source. The source problem is competitive thought, which is a virus infection of the brain.

First you must realize that you have a virus, and second you begin to play with the virus removal tool: to speak, act and think more cooperatively, and to celebrate everything about everyone.

When people have performance issues, you help them move to the kind of structure that lets them excel. There still has to be accountability. There still has to be individual output. People still have to step up to the bar for excellence. We just need to teach our children.

If you teach 3- to 5-year-olds cooperative theory, you get them so they don't speak, say or do anything that takes magnificence away from another spiritual being. You're going to have people walk in occasionally and do very bad things like we hear about in the news, but that's a competitive thinker. That's a damaged brain.

We all can begin to remove the core damages. The violence that we're seeing today in our news is because so many brains have been infected by the competitive virus, and we are seeing the output of that virus. There's nothing cooperative about what's going on. Once you step back into the solution, how to get out of the pain they're suffering, you get into cooperative dynamics of celebration.

Q: As you're saying, the shift is happening. It's happening, it seems, because the collaborative model is the one that works and everything else is crumbling.

If you just want bottom-line results, you've got to reform your organizational model in the workplace away from competitive systems, communications, recognition and reward systems and get a new model. It's very easy to put in. It's fast once you get a cooperative culture change. You tell the employees, "We're going to move from competition to cooperation." They get switched on just by that.

Q: Do you still see competitive people who are clinging to the old ways, who still want to be top dog and may be afraid that if they go collaborative, they will lose their positioning?

There are those that you cannot train. They have to exit. They have to go back into competitive, toxic soup and stay there because they want to live in that environment.

Once you really wake up to cooperative thinking and cooperative friends, family and associations, you just find competitive thinkers and problem-solvers to be boring. They don't have any power or passion. You think of it as a form of ignorance like any prejudice.

You see it as a virus. You feel bad for them because you know they're infected. They don't want to remove the virus. And you don't want to be around the virus anymore.

Once you remove your own viruses, it's like the veil coming off your eyes. If we take it religiously, in all the literature you basically have an Eternal Being, God, making free will. One of the creatures is in competition with God, saying, "I exist on my own life-force separate from Your life-force. I am not dependent on You. I am separate from You and I am as powerful as You."

That thought is insane. It's the virus that started it all, that kind of divisional virus. We are all united children, babies of a Divine Entity, and the Parent is nuts about us. The Parent loves the children. Yet we constantly run away from the love. It's time to turn around and just open our arms. It doesn't take a lot of effort. Just stop running.

Q: The United Nations distinguishes between peacemaking, peacekeeping and peacebuilding. Our focus is primarily on peacebuilders, people who are creating environments and cultures where peace can thrive.

First, we've developed CEO Space Nation (*www.ceospacenation.com*). The website shows a video about the program we are bringing to governments.

Governments are buying an economic recovery program to stimulate permanent growth for their economies in Africa, and in developing countries all over Asia. As they put these programs to work, we organize all of the entrepreneurial activity for the largest companies, the midsize companies and those starting up on cooperative theory thousands at a time. They go out as the virus removal tool into those societies. They become the leaders and the financial empire-builders.

They're all doing it cooperatively, collaboratively, and it doesn't leave a lot of room for competition. Competition as an idea is a thought-form that is dying. And like all thought forms when they die, they fight for their life.

An example is terrorism. Terrorism is the ultimate hatred and competition. There's no authority for the Taliban. It doesn't have an authority. It's not trying to do something religiously. It's not trying to do something politically. It's just power. It's only power, so it has no sense of a balance. It's the ultimate form of the virus and when you look at it, it becomes very boring.

The way to get rid of it, by the way, is actually not to use bullets, but to cooperate with it to get into discussions because then you can change its mind.

You have to work with the mind of the infected. You can't shoot it all. I mean that's not going to solve the problem. The virus communicates wirelessly and we have to exercise our new ways of dealing with the virus. I think illumination is the first weapon.

Q: What is your vision? Imagine we're living in a 100 percent collaborative world. What does the world look like?

It looks like the rapture. It looks like a fifth dimensionalized planet in which we have moved in a blink of an eye to a higher energy dimension. We don't have the sense of ownership we used to have for each other. We stay on the planet for thousands of years. We discover the stars. We clean up our Earth in an easy way. We become fascinated with learning and have the kind of discoveries we've always been made for. We get closer and closer to the Source as we are given increasing revelations to discover the mind of God. Constant discovery and exploration. It's the most exciting time of humanity. It's the last great revolution.

If we don't become cooperative, the planet will shrug us off because the planet is alive and cooperative. It cooperates with itself, and it will shrug us off like fleas and make a new breed. If we cooperate, we can have the most exciting exploration that's ever happened in the history of consciousness. And if we don't cooperate, we'll use our weapons and the planet will start again.

Q: Do you see it happening?

I think there is a divine plan. I think it is perfect and it will play out in that divine way. We are all elements of this. The peacemakers are coming onto the planet at this time and you can feel them. You feel them when they walk in a room.

You'll know when Dr. John Demartini walks in the room. You'll know it when Lisa Nichols walks in the room. They shouldn't have to say anything. They are the great peacemakers. They are collaborationalists. They're cooperationalists. They understand. They don't speak or do anything that takes away magnificence from another being's journey.

Q: What is your personal practice for staying centered in a state of peace?

Five times a year, we come together with thousands of business owners, and talk, act and practice cooperation. It is a set of practices that we think is more important than golf or hang gliding. So we spend five times a year together and we nurture cooperative practices. All the businesses thrive. We win awards in all categories. Everybody has better results, and more and more get attracted in because they see, "My gosh, these guys are hiring during a recession! These guys are doing great. How are they doing that?"

You never have more than 60 days in the toxic soup of competition before you go back to the oasis of tens of thousands of people who are now doing their business life in cooperation.

*****

B.J. Dohrmann is a world change agent, advising CEOs of the largest industries, as well as heads of state. His Sovereign Nation Program complements the five World Trade Shows Dohrmann produces each year for industrial CEOs and their management (*www.ceospace.net*), with "in nation" training for economic development of participating host countries (*www.ceospacenation.com*). Dohrmann's book *The Cooperative Revolution: Redemption* defines the death of the first generation of competitive capitalism with all of its abuses and the birth of the future of cooperative, collaborative capitalism, which is the next generation of capitalism.

*****

Reflection Points:

Reflect on your own work environment. On a scale of 1 to 10 (with 10 being the most competitive), how competitive do you perceive your field to be?

In what ways could you conceivably collaborate with your "competition"? How could you bring more collaborative practices into your business life and career?

The Peacebuilder Challenge:

Identify a person or team that could be perceived as competition. Invite them to join you to brainstorm ways you can leverage your experiences to help them be more successful. Seek only to give your support and share your resources (set aside any hidden outcomes for personal gain) and notice what happens!

8

ATTRACTING PEACE AND ABUNDANCE

Joe Vitale

Joe Vitale is a man who is putting principles into practice to create a world of financial abundance for all people. Joe explains the connection between peace and prosperity, and demonstrates through his life's example how a paradigm of inner peace creates the building blocks for outer wealth and financial mastery.

> "Get out of your ego and make a difference in the world. Help bring peace by practicing peace in your own life, and contributing to the things you believe in."
>
> —Joe Vitale, author of *Zero Limits* and *The Attractor Factor*

Q: Many of us know you as a spiritual teacher, particularly when it comes to manifesting money and creating abundance. Tell us why you think these teachings are so important when it comes to creating a world of peace.

Right now, most people aren't very peaceful. They're in struggle. They're in desperation. They are hurting. They are hungry. It doesn't take much asking around among family and friends to find out how many people have lost their jobs, have lost their homes, or are in fear of one or the other.

Money, finances, security. Fear is very much on their mind, and when it is, they are not at peace. So I want to help them.

I've done it for friends and family, and I've been doing it through coaching programs. But I want to do it in a bigger way.

I'm actually giving away my book *Attract Money Now* because I really feel that people have to find inner peace within themselves, and once they do, that ripple effect will start taking place so that we can see it across the planet.

This is practical metaphysics for me. It's the kind that you take to the bank. Unless people get their mindset around this and take care of their money, their finances, and, of course, their worries and concerns, they're not going to feel peaceful.

Q: So it's like peace is the cause and abundance is the effect?

Is that ever a great line! Can I quote that? That is good.

Abundance is an inside job and money will match your mindset. If you have a mindset of worry, concern or anything that's not peaceful, then you're actually going to be attracting experiences, more feelings and more outer results to match that lack of peace. You've got to have the peace to begin with.

Once you do, everything else, the security, the money and the other things that you look for in the material world, starts to come into your world. But it begins with this inner sense of tranquility.

Q: It seems that's the real challenge then. Poverty becomes one of those cycles that can be so easy to get stuck in. As you said, everyone's worried. Everyone's anxious because "the money's not there" and so we create more of "the money's not there." How do you break out of that cycle?

I was homeless in Dallas about 35 years ago. I lived in poverty for the longest time. My mindset was such that I was not very peaceful, and as I looked around, I was not very relaxed.

As I interpreted what I was seeing, I saw lack and limitation. The world was against me. I didn't have much hope, and as a result of that, I kept attracting more things to reinforce my beliefs.

What I tell people is that we're in a belief-driven universe. A change of beliefs will get a different reality. You'll start to experience peace. You'll start to attract peace. It all has to happen on the inside.

Q: Joe, you speak about the Law of Attraction in the movie The Secret. *I think most of us have seen that movie and know the power of the Law of Attraction that we've been talking about. What is it that sparks your passion for teaching people how to attract abundance?*

My big insight that I want everybody to get is that the Law of Attraction is working on the unconscious beliefs within you. It's not working on the conscious beliefs. This is where a lot of people get confused, because they'll say, "I watched *The Secret* and I practiced the Law of Attraction," "I'm trying to find peace," or "I'm trying to attract money, and it's not happening!"

Most of the time, it's not happening because of what you're unconsciously thinking, not what you're consciously thinking. Consciously, you can think, *The Secret* is great, the Law of Attraction is great, Joe Vitale is great, Mindy is great. I'm going to attract money and I'm doing everything I can think of to make that happen.

But unconsciously, you think, I don't deserve it. I'm not lovable, I'm not smart enough, I'm not good enough, or Money is bad, money is evil, rich people are greedy. If I have a lot of money, my family and friends will attack us all, and come and take it from me. If you have any sort of these negative, limiting beliefs in your unconscious mind, you will sabotage your own best efforts.

Most people who are not at peace right now have unconscious issues they're wrestling with, and most people have the belief that they're not worth loving.

If they have that in their unconscious mind because of conclusions they made as they were growing up and so forth, then they're not going to be at peace. They have to take care of that, and this is what excites me. Once you delve into this, it is not a big deal. It's not that hard. You can take care of it.

When you do take care of the inside, then you find peace. Then you attract the things that you consciously say you want. Then you are more in the deep, divine flow of life.

Q: What are your own personal practices that you use to stay in that feeling space of peace?

I wrote a book called *Zero Limits,* and in it, there's a four-phrase mantra that a therapist used to heal an entire ward of mentally ill criminals. I use those four phrases all the time, including right now. I've made it my new self-talk.

Instead of having the talk that most of us have in our brain that puts us down, second-guesses us, doubts us, and so forth, these four phrases are based on love. The phrases are "I love you," "I'm sorry," "Please forgive me," and "Thank you."

Even if you just reduced it to "I love you" and you end up saying that in your mind all the time, you will start to achieve peace.

If there's any takeaway point that I can give people, Mindy, it is the idea that if you change your self-talk, you will change your inner vibe and you can do it as easily as saying, "I love you" mentally to yourself.

You don't have to say it out loud, though that would be interesting if you did. As you change yourself, you will experience inner peace. You will clean and clear the negativity, the limiting beliefs, and as you experience the inner peace, you will start to see outer peace.

As each person does this, the collective consciousness gets shifted and then we suddenly see peace on a global scale. But it all begins individually, and for me, "I love you" is the secret password to begin to go there.

Q: *Well, I love you, Joe. I love the conversation. And I love the idea and the principle, because it goes back to ancient wisdom. All the great spiritual teachings, regardless of what religion it is, boil down to that one idea of love expressed, as you said, through forgiveness and apology. It's all gratitude. It's all love.*

It really is. You mentioned forgiveness. That's another great technique. Forgiving yourself and forgiving others is a great way to go right into peace.

I saw the ending to an old movie from the 1990s last night, *Flatliners*. Kiefer Sutherland, Kevin Bacon and some others are in there, and it's about these medical doctors who are experimenting with death. They put themselves into death for a minute or so and then come back.

Then they start to get troubled by their past until they realize what they have to do is atone. They have to forgive themselves. They don't have to do it with anybody else. They can do it inside themselves. They can do it mentally. It's like forgiving themselves or anybody they perceive had done some sort of wrong to them. They find peace within themselves.

I thought, What a profound movie! The bottom-line message was forgiveness, with a direct message about creating peace in this moment.

Q: Beautiful. Joe, we think of you as the guru when it comes to spiritual marketing, prosperity, abundance. I also know that you have a real passion for helping people. You have an organization called Operation Y.E.S. (Your Economic Solution). Tell us what the vision is for Operation Y.E.S.

Operation Y.E.S. is designed to end homelessness in this country. As I mentioned earlier, I was homeless at one point and in poverty for the longest time, so I know what it feels like. I know the sting. I used to not even talk about it, because it's fairly traumatic, at least psychologically, and of course, embarrassing.

So I've put together a group of people, and I'm starting to work with another program called Circles that plans to end poverty. They've already worked with 1,000 families in the United States. I want to help people on at least three levels.

The first is to take care of self-esteem issues. As I mentioned earlier, most people who are struggling with money or worried about finances, their home or security, are not at peace. They've got to find that inner peace before anything else starts to work for them. So I want to teach them some clearing methods, if you will, from psychological self-help methods to help them love themselves, to help them find inner strength and self-worth.

Too many people who have been homeless, myself included, start to feel that they are worthless and that life is hopeless. At that point, you don't have much of a chance, so you have to get your head around possibility thinking. You and I know how powerful that is, but somebody who's been kicked in the gut financially doesn't really accept that.

So the first step in Operation Y.E.S. is to help people understand that they are lovable, that they are loved, that they are valued, and that they are valuable. We help them get their mindset healthy again.

Then I want to start teaching them that if they start thinking like an entrepreneur, they will have a better chance of attracting money, because too many of us give our power away. We want another job, a better job, a different location or a different wage, but we're giving our power away.

I'm not saying jobs are bad, but I am saying if you think like an entrepreneur, you see more opportunities around you. Then you begin to realize that any problem that you hear is an opportunity for a product or service that you can create.

Of course there's more to it, but I want to teach everybody that goes into Operation Y.E.S. how to think like this. It's not a big deal. I didn't think like an entrepreneur when I was growing up or when I was homeless. I had to learn how to do this. Now my mind can't turn that off. I see opportunities everywhere.

Then the third level is to put that business online. The Internet has leveled the field. Anybody can go online. Even if you don't have a computer, you can go into the library and borrow a computer long enough to set up a website, do research or even read my free book *Attract Money Now*. Do it online at the library.

I want people to realize if they think like an entrepreneur, they think that they love themselves and that they deserve success, and they start to experiment with selling things online, then they can pull themselves up, find inner peace, start to attract money and attract prosperity. As a result of that, they can help other people do the same thing, much like I do.

If I remained homeless, I wouldn't be able to help anybody right now. But because I've gotten out of that and gone way beyond it, I'm now in a position where I can help people find peace and prosperity. That excites me beyond belief.

Q: I can tell! Joe, talk about what peace means to you.

It's an inner sense of tranquility. It ends up being something you have to subjectively find for yourself. It's a sense inside yourself of imperturbability. It's a sense of deep relaxation, acceptance and love with yourself and your surroundings.

Peace, for me, is that tranquil state. I'm visualizing a lake that just has a smoothness to it because there is no drama, there is no upset and there is nothing going on within it. It is this inner sense of nonjudgment of life.

Q: What is your vision for what you think humanity can create on this planet?

What humanity could create is something that would be beyond my ego's description. I would be putting a limitation on it.

I can give you this example. Years ago, back in Houston, I gave a talk in a small church. There might have been 20 people in the room, and I walked in with a jigsaw puzzle. I took it and passed it around. I asked everybody to take one piece. So there are 20 people in the room and they were all holding a piece of the jigsaw puzzle.

As they look at their piece, they don't know what to do with it. They don't know what it contributes to, and they don't know what the end picture is. But I held up the board that it came from, the cover of the box, and I said, "When all of us contribute our individual piece, we end up making this beautiful painting."

That's how it will be with peace on Earth, each of us following our passion and our calling, and making that contribution. Sharing our piece of the puzzle.

Q: *I love it. So how do we bridge the gap from here to there?*

It's an inside job. We can't go out and change other people. What we need to do is work on ourselves. As I take care of myself, and you take care of yourself, we begin to live that piece of the puzzle that exudes peace.

Instead of trying to change the world with persuasion techniques, I'd rather be an inspiration. I'd rather be an example.

So when people hear that Joe Vitale was homeless at one point, but now Joe Vitale is in 13 movies, on *Larry King Live*, and traveling around the world, they can see that they can change too. They can have a different life. Whatever they're experiencing right now, as I say in my book *The Attractor Factor*, is just current reality and current reality will change as long as you participate with it from the inside-out.

Tune in to yourself. Learn to meditate. Practice the I-love-yous and follow your passion, your calling, the thing that you would do whether you were paid for it or not. All of this is exuding from a place of peace within you.

As you exude that and live that, it will inspire others. That will contribute to the global consciousness. Other people will see it and say, "Wow! If they can do it, I can do it too."

Q: *In your book* Attract Money **Now**, *you write about a formula for attracting money. Does that formula apply to attracting peace?*

Absolutely. The very first step has a lot to do with our unconscious beliefs.

Peace begins within ourselves. We have to come from a place of peace, otherwise we don't see clearly life itself. We won't see our choices. We won't see our opportunities. We look around and we will just see danger everywhere.

When you come from peace, you realize you are safe. You are love. You are loving. And you exude that sense of trust with each breath that you take.

Then you see the opportunities around you. You can feel the Divine nudging you. You can see the business ideas, if that happens to be the case.

Of course, the book is about attracting money; but for me, money is only a symbol. Money is not the big deal that everybody makes it out to be. It's just paper and ink. It's coin. It's metal. We project meaning onto it and often the meaning we project is not very peaceful.

We see it as a kind of life raft. We see it as our saving grace. It is the thing that is going to make life all better. That's not a peaceful mindset. That's a desperate mindset. Inner peace is where this all begins.

Q: *What is one thing that we can do to experience greater financial peace?*

I think this will tie in to everything we've been talking about. It's one of the seven steps in the book *Attract Money Now*. It is the idea of contributing to a cause, to people or a movement that you believe in.

In other words, get out of your ego. Too many people are shut down with their possibilities for income or even peace because they are totally focused on themselves. I learned a long time ago that when you really believe in something—for example, Operation Y.E.S., the *Circles* program I mentioned, or it could be the Red Cross, your local church, anything—whatever it is, go and contribute time, money and energy. Do whatever you can to make a difference there. It's going to expand your own mindset. It's going to get you out of your ego and the universe will karmically bless you by doing this.

Get out of your ego and make a difference in the world. Help bring peace about by practicing peace in your own life, and contributing to the things you believe in.

*****

Joe Vitale (*www.joevitale.com*) is president of Hypnotic Marketing, Inc., a marketing consulting firm. He has been called the "Buddha of the Internet" for his combination of spirituality and marketing acumen. His books include *Zero Limits*, *The Attractor Factor*, and *Attract Money Now* (the free book download is available when you opt-in at *www.attractmoneynow.com*). He is also one of the stars of the hit movie *The Secret* and the founder of Operation Y.E.S. (*www.operationyes.com*), an organization dedicated to eliminating homelessness in America.

*****

Reflection Points

What are the thoughts and beliefs that you notice when you think about your finances?

On a scale of 1 to 10, how peaceful do you feel about your current financial situation (with 10 being fully at peace)?

The Peacebuilder Challenge

Make a list of the gifts and talents that you recognize in yourself that would be valuable to share with others. Brainstorm services that you could offer to others based on these gifts. (For example: Write an article for their newsletter, organize a fundraising event, or cook something delicious for their volunteers, et cetera) Then choose a nonprofit organization that inspires you and volunteer your talents or financial resources to support a short- or long-term project. This could include schools, civic groups or nonprofit organizations in your community.

9

QUANTUM PEACE

Garland Landrith

Garland Landrith, Ph.D., was the first to publish a research study in a scientific journal about how the thoughts of individuals doing transcendental meditation can influence the outer world by reducing things like crimes, auto accidents and even suicides. He is a faculty adviser for the Global Peace Project and joins us to discuss ways of establishing peace in every cell of our body.

> "If we're going to change the outside world, we've got to change the inside world. We have to stop those fearful subconscious thoughts that are cropping up and biting us in the back."
> —Garland Landrith, *The Universe Lies Within*

Q: *Peace is one of those subjects that I think sometimes people are afraid to talk about. World peace: It sounds so big and distant. It's almost as if people are afraid of being too Pollyanna about it, or seeming like an idealist, all "butterflies-and-lollipops." What does peace look like through the eyes of a quantum scientist?*

We all want peace, but the wanting of peace doesn't seem to be making much of a difference. We all have good intentions. We all have very powerful positive thoughts, but they don't seem to be hitting with the *oomph* that we want.

Researcher Dean Radin describes a very intriguing experiment in his book *The Conscious Universe*. This hits home the real essence of the problem: Researchers gathered a bunch of people and had them guess whether a photograph on a computer screen would be negative or positive. The negative photographs were really negative. It showed people in morgues. Because the photo was so gruesome, researchers anticipated that there would be an increase in tension. So they hooked them up to Galvanic Skin Response machines, which are similar to lie-detector tests. What they found was that people couldn't guess what was going to come up on the screen.

But luckily, these lie-detector machines were going on during the whole experiment. They found what they expected: an increase in tension every time the gruesome photo was presented. Well, they did indeed find that tension increased, but it happened two seconds *before* the negative photo was presented.

Q: *Before they saw the photo, the body responded?*

Right. In other words, the study participants knew what was going to happen before it happened. They replicated this study in Europe, and they also looked at the MRIs. The whole brain would light up with anxiety about four seconds before the actual photo was presented.

This research study indicates that our body seems to have a quantum type connection that allows it to know what is going to happen before our mind does. By "quantum," I mean that it has knowledge beyond the time-space limitations that are present in our normal day-to-day living.

This study tells us that our body energies have somehow got to be reconnected with our minds to add more oomph to our positive thoughts. That means *techniques* matter more than *intentions* because we need to find a way to reconnect our consciousness with our quantum Nature, which is beyond the time-space limitations.

Q: *This opens up some pretty big questions. So how do we create peace? Is peace something that we can create if our body is responding to something subconsciously?*

That's the key. The problem is not our conscious-thinking mind, but our subconscious mind. All those things that happened to us when we were little, when we were in the womb, before we were born, they have an influence on what we think. Our conscious mind is really being determined by our subconscious mind, which is full of doubts and fears.

Q: *So if we have the idea that we're not worthy, that the world is a dangerous place, or that any of those types of beliefs are swimming around in our body energy, what do we do? How do we turn that around?*

You can say, "Okay, I'll just think positive thoughts," but if our conscious mind is being determined by the subconscious, thinking positive thoughts is not really going to change things that well.

We've got to do something to change the actual subconscious mind and the window into the subconscious is through the body. Through the Peace Project, I have taught hundreds and hundreds of people how to tap on acupuncture points. Then I also taught them how to get to the quantum field, kind of mixing acupuncture with quantum technology. You can meditate with it. You can pray with it. You can manifest with it. That's what we did.

I am not saying that intentions are not important. What I am saying is that letting go of the intention is far more important than thinking the intention.

I will tell you a little secret. In the movie *What the Bleep Do We Know?* they referenced a study where 4,000 transcendental meditators went to Washington, D.C., to change the crime levels. More than 4,000 of us were there. We spent eight hours a day in deep meditation. Never once did we think about crimes. All we did was go there and meditate.

So the intention is not the most important thing. In fact, in a study where I was one of the primary authors, we found the effect without any intention at all. This study was published in the *International Journal of Neuroscience*.

We measured the brainwaves of people who were meditating in Iowa while a rather large meditation course with more than 2,000 participants was going on in Amherst, Massachusetts. We found that when people were meditating in Amherst, Massachusetts, it would influence the brainwaves of people in Iowa.

What made this study really amazing was that the people in Amherst did not even know that they were in a study, so there was absolutely no intention involved.

Likewise, the meditators in Iowa were not told the true reason for the study until after it was over. We proposed that what was going on was a kind of collective consciousness field effect that would radiate outward and influence the surrounding area.

Q: *Okay, so you start with the intention and then you just release it.*

Release it. Releasing it makes it infinitely more powerful, and at the same time getting the body energies aligned with your mind.

Q: *Now you said you lead people to the quantum field. Let's back-track a little bit and talk about what that means.*

Electrons are in the quantum. They are everywhere all at the same time. There are no boundaries. They break every law of nature. But if you try to measure them, they appear and are bound by time and space. So, to get to the quantum, we've got to learn to let go and be in that field where we are everywhere all at the same time so that we have maximum impact. That means letting go of all of our thoughts, feelings and perceptions so they are in a quantum field of infinite possibilities.

When the electron is in the normal state, it is bound by the laws of time and space. When we have an intention, we are bound by the normal time-space continuum. But when we are in the quantum field, we are beyond the time-space boundaries so our intentions can manifest abundance without limitations.

Q: *Connect the dots for us. What's the connection between access-ing the quantum field and creating a world of peace?*

When you change your own mind so that it's connecting with everything in creation, your thoughts merge with every-body else's thoughts and you have more power with everyone else. Also, you have a lot more peace inside because with peace, if we're going to change the outside world, we've got to change the inside world. We've got to stop those fearful subconscious thoughts that are cropping up and biting us in the back, because really when you think about it, we all want the same thing.

We all want peace. We all want a world that works for everybody. Everybody wants the same thing. People just want to grow up, have their own kids and do their own thing.

Q: So why is it so difficult? Why has it never been done before on a planetary level?

It's because the inner peace is not there within us. Everybody is afraid. There are people who are afraid that we're going to hurt them, and people who are afraid they are going to hurt us. The fears are in the subconscious, so we're not aware of the fears. We are just aware of our wants and desires.

That is the key. We've got to change the subconscious body energies and that means changing the flow inside our bodies. That's what we've found. By tapping on acupuncture points— this is the Emotional Freedom Technique (EFT) that I do— mixed with the quantum meditations, it actually produces an effect inside the body that makes magical things happen. People get jobs when there are no jobs. People sell houses when everybody can't sell a house. Things just happen.

Q: What progress have you seen already in the time that you've been working with this project?

Over a 10-month period working with The Global Peace Project in Dallas, Texas, with only about 1,000 people doing these Quantum Tapping Techniques, there was a 20 percent reduction in the city's crime rate.

Q: *This within the first 10 months?*

Yes, and this is what makes it even more huge: It occurred during a recession, when crime rates typically go up. So this is a huge, huge development.

Q: *How does that individual person doing their individual practice impact a city as large as the city of Dallas?*

The TM (Transcendental Meditation) people have replicated this in over 40 studies. This was the first time anyone tried this with Tapping (EFT), and we found the same results as they did with meditation. So the Peace Project in Dallas was the first to suggest that Tapping can do the same thing as meditation.

I'll tell you about some of the peace projects the TM people did as well.

Tony Nader, M.D., Ph.D., conducted a series of studies in Lebanon. This is years ago when the Lebanon War was going on. They brought in 350 people. That wasn't enough people, so they brought another 150 which brought them to 500, which was one percent of the population of the town being instructed in the Transcendental Meditation Program. According to the research, there was an immediate end to hostilities and an improvement in social, economic and ecological conditions in the town, a sharp contrast to the continuing violence in surrounding areas

Q: *Garland, we've been talking about the inner process of peace. What happens when people come together with a common intention in the name of peace?*

The big mystery is "Why does letting go of the intention work better than the intention itself?" Really, in order to understand that, we've got to understand the quantum field, because the quantum field basically has two sides to it.

There's a side that is called the *vacuum state* which means *nothing*. But obviously, it's not nothing, because nothing couldn't create everything. So they like to think of it as an unmanifest wave function waiting to manifest. In other words, it's like a virtual something going on, but we don't know what that virtual something is. It's something, but it looks like nothing, tastes like nothing, and has the appearance of being nothing. It's potential waiting to manifest.

The quantum inside our minds is the same thing. It's the state without thoughts, feelings or perceptions. You've got to learn to let go of the intention in order to make the intention get into the quantum, so that the intention can have more force behind it. That's the intriguing dilemma, because we normally think if we have a stronger intention then we should be able to have a stronger effect.

That's the reason why, when I talked to Donna Collins with The Global Peace Project, I said, "We have to emphasize technique because techniques will help us learn to let go. Then our body energies will be aligned with our mind. Then the whole thing will happen without spending all this time on intentions." When you try too hard, it never works. It's like trying to hit a golf ball. It doesn't work.

Q: *You've got to let go and breathe. Find your perfect sweet spot, right?*

Right. You've got to get into the flow.

Q: *What is one practical, easy thing that we can do here in our physical reality to help create this vision of peace in the world?*

I think the best thing a person can do to create peace is to learn how to tap on their body energy systems with their fingers with a process like EFT (Emotional Freedom Technique). It's tapping on acupuncture points. When I teach it, it's called "quantum tapping." Especially when you combine it with other techniques of meditation, you actually learn how to get the body energies relaxed so that you get into the meditative state. You get into that state of manifestation much more easily instead of having the monkey-mind that's going all over the place. Your mind learns how to let go and flow, and that energy flows along with it.

Q: *Every time you say, "Let go of the intention," it presupposes that there is an intention to begin with. Does the clarity or the focus of that intention seem to have an effect on the manifestation?*

I'd say the strongest manifestation is just sending love while being in a state of gratitude. When you are in the state of gratitude, you attract more things to be grateful for.

A lot of people would disagree with that. A lot of people say you've got to be very specific about what you want. I have found that when you're less specific, you actually seem to get it easier because you are more open to other possible ways to get what you want.

Let's say you want abundance. You're thinking in terms of money and you think, I'm just going to send love towards abundance. I'm not going to worry about the details. You might end up with the job of your dreams, and you are abundant in ways you've never dreamed before because you are abundant inside, you're flowing, you're happy, and you don't even realize you're working. Abundance can come so many different ways.

I take the position that being less specific is more important. It lets the divine flow of nature help you get where you want to be, and when you have the divine flow of nature behind you, it gets a lot easier to get there than if you're trying to make the divine flow go in your way.

Q: *It's sort of the difference between "my will" and "Thy will."*

Exactly. Beautifully said.

Everything that we're talking about here—peace, abundance, happiness, joy—all of those things seem to be our natural state, so it just makes sense that we would manifest these as we release and let go.

Q: *What message would you want future generations to know about peace from your perspective right here and now?*

It can become a reality if we do the techniques. We can create the world of our dreams. There's no doubt about it.

Just do the techniques. You've got to do them every day. Twice a day or three times a day and you will change the world. We have proven it now with numerous studies. There is no doubt we can create miracles in our mind.

*****

Dr. Garland Landrith (*www.theuniverselieswithin.com*) is a cutting-edge quantum field psychologist and energy healer whose research was cited in the highly acclaimed film *What the Bleep Do We Know?* He was among the first to scientifically document that "what we think inside can have a profound influence on the outer world." In his pioneering research studies published in 1981, 1982 and 1988, it was found that what individuals think in group meditations can improve the quality of life in the cities they live in by lowering crime rates, auto accidents and suicides. In short, we can create miracles in our outer worlds with our own minds.

*****

Reflection Points

Bring to mind your intentions for your life and for the world. What if you released all attachment to these outcomes?

What are the beliefs and fears that may be preventing you from fulfilling your intentions?

The Peacebuilder Challenge

Explore the basics of the Emotional Freedom Technique (EFT) method Dr. Landrith describes. You can receive information about how to use this technique by clicking on the "Get Started Free" link at *www.eftuniverse.com* or search for Dr. Landrith on YouTube to access his free introductory videos.

10

REACHING IN

Lynne Brown

Rev. Lynne Brown is vice president of Silent Unity, a 24/7 prayer ministry established in 1890. As a leader and organizer of World Day of Prayer, Lynne talked about the power of prayer and the importance of "reaching in" to connect with the Source of true and lasting peace.

> "To be focused on Spirit, on the Divine, on God the Good—whatever term of endearment you give to the Higher Power—really moves you to that place of peace."
>
> —Rev. Lynne Brown, Silent Unity

Q: Silent Unity has provided free prayer services for people around the world for more than 100 years. To begin, tell us why Unity founders Charles and Myrtle Fillmore used prayer as the foundation for the Unity movement.

Prayer was central to their own transformation. The beginning of our Unity movement was the result of healings they experienced in their lives, and they shared about these experiences in their writings. As they shared spiritual principles and practices with individuals, prayer was core. It was central to their very life experience and to their transformation.

It continues to be that today, Mindy, as we have an opportunity to serve thousands of people a day by providing affirmative prayer support. Prayer makes a difference. It changes lives and in lasting ways.

Q: It's true. There is so much healing, whether it's in an economic sense or in terms of relationships, pain, suffering, health—all the different things that draw us into prayer. Of course, we know that it doesn't need to be a response to suffering. How can we use prayer as a tool in every area of our life?

Moving through this human life experience, we can find situations that create maybe small, minor or major hiccups in our daily lives.

We need to be reminded that while we're in this human experience, we are spiritual beings. We need to take the opportunity to pause—a very sacred pause in the activity of prayer—to recenter ourselves, to refocus, and to realign our thoughts with the Divine. Love this life journey in every way, but do so in an awareness of the Divine Presence within. We nurture this awareness and bring it into expression through the sacred practice of affirmative prayer.

Q: Tell us a little bit about what is unique about Unity's style of prayer.

It's powerful and it's effective. It's essentially a practice, a method, an approach to prayer that our founders found to be very effective. Affirmative prayer, as it states, is affirmative. It's positive. My comments are not intended to judge the way others pray, but affirmative prayer is not a method of beseeching or begging.

In Unity, we're not praying as a means of influencing God or persuading God to do more. We believe that God is All. As spiritual beings, we are one with God. We live, move and have our being in the presence of God. We pray with the intention of being open and receptive to divine goodness everywhere present and at the very center of our being. Affirmative prayer is positive, recognizing the good, claiming it and demonstrating it as spiritual qualities in our daily lives.

Q: Each year, Silent Unity participates in World Day of Prayer. Talk about the significance of that day.

Unity World Day of Prayer is an annual event at Unity Village. We invite all participants to focus on the One Presence and the One Power within our lives, within all lives, and within the universe in a 24-hour prayer vigil and other sacred activities. Many Unity churches host a 24-hour event or hold prayer activities during the day. We know and believe that minds and hearts aligned with focused prayer energy make a positive difference in the consciousness of our world.

Q: Talk about that, because I think that's a really significant piece of the World Day of Prayer experience. There is a global coming together in prayer. Talk about why that's so powerful.

On World Day of Prayer, there are nearly 1 million people around the world united in prayerful thought and spiritual focus. I know that it touches people's lives because we hear the stories. There is something very sacred about the energy of prayer, and it is felt on that day with that many minds and hearts linked in prayerful connectedness.

Q: I think it's perfect that World Day of Prayer precedes International Day of Peace. They are about two weeks apart. It seems like such a great reflection of how peace actually is manifested. It begins in prayer and then it takes form in our lives and in our world. What can people who want to participate in World Day of Prayer be doing now to get ready for this big day?

I invite anyone who is interested to go to *www.worlddayof-prayer.org* and learn about all the ways to participate. The whole emphasis is on prayer, on reaching in and allowing divine wisdom to inspire us, guide us, and moves us in reaching out. We're inviting the world to act. Reach in as you pray with us. Reach out as you're guided in making a difference in your life, in one another's lives, and in the lives of people around the world. It's transformational, and we can rock the world in a very positive, life-changing way together.

Q: *I agree. It is very exciting to reach in and reach out. I know that people can reach out in service, and they can also reach out in prayer. Lynne, what is your vision for a world of peace and what part does prayer play in that vision?*

The very practice of affirmative prayer—a focus on God's infinite goodness within ourselves and within all people—moves people instantly. To be focused on Spirit, on the Divine, on God the Good—whatever term of endearment you give to the Higher Power—to align your thoughts with Truth, with the Presence and in Divine Knowing, really moves you to that place of peace.

As our master teacher, Jesus Christ, talked about, "peace not as the world gives, but as I give." The peace of the Divine is within each one of us. It's always present. We bring the Divine into our conscious awareness, and we do that in prayer.

That's really what this book, *Let It Begin With Me*, is all about. It's hearing these leading-edge voices that are inviting us into conscious awareness and into a world of peace.

Q: To reach in, know, feel and experience peace is truly where peace on a global scale begins. Lynne, what is the image of peace that you hold?

I see it every day. Children so beautifully express love and peace. I see it in the eyes of children. Not to say that we adults don't express peace, but maybe not quite as freely as a child.

We can learn from children, and we can let that be our invitation to express the peace that is our natural state. Nature itself, for me, is an expression of and an invitation to live in peace, beauty and order, and not to get caught up in the temporary situations and circumstances of everyday life. There's a natural beauty and order that is always present.

When we can remember to see the beauty and to align with the flow of Spirit, peace is our experience—it is our natural state. It's what we feel. It's what we express. Prayer invites us to reconnect with the divine essence of our being.

Q: I agree. Lynne, how do we use that awareness and that clarity that we experience in prayer so we can identify our gifts and reach out in service to the world?

The beauty of prayer is that peace is constant and wisdom is instantly accessible. We become still and allow ourselves to move to that centered place within.

As we quietly pause, focus our thoughts, prayerfully reflect and truly listen, we hear the still small voice. For some, it can be audible. For most of us, it is an intuitive knowing. Divine ideas come to our awareness in the silence of prayer. We realize divine ideas and then we take action to put feet on our prayers. In prayer, we know what to do, there is clarity, and we are moved to put the ideas into motion.

Q: *Lynne, I love it when you pray. Would you be willing to help us all reach in as you share with us a prayer for inner peace? Could you lead us in prayer?*

I would love to, Mindy.

I invite you to take a deep, cleansing breath, and let your body relax. Whatever activities await you, let it be for now. For in this moment, we choose to take a sacred pause.

Gently move your attention from outer activities to the Divine Presence within you—that which is constant and eternal. The very act of turning our attention within centers us in peace—inner peace. It is always present within us. I invite you to feel the presence of Divine Love throughout your being.

No angst. No concerns. No thoughts beyond this moment, beyond the Sacred, the Divine. It's a beautiful presence. It's instantly accessible, surrounding us, within us. It is the peace that is ever-present and lasting. It is the peace that transforms our lives and changes the world for the better.

In this presence of peace, we surrender. We allow our awareness to be lifted to that consciousness of peace that is lasting, knowing this truth for our own lives, for the lives of those we love, for our world family. We bring forth an image of peace for those that we know and for those we don't know.

We visualize peace in their choices, in their actions, and in their relationships. We see each one awakening more fully to this peace that is constant within them. For this truth, for this awareness in which we unite, for this oneness that is our eternal connection, for the peace that is lasting, we say, "Thank you, Spirit." And so it is. Amen.

*****

Rev. Lynne Brown is an ordained Unity minister and serves as vice president of Silent Unity and Development. Silent Unity celebrated 120 years of service in 2010. The prayer ministry is accessible 24 hours a day, seven days a week, and receives nearly 2 million prayer requests each year from people of many different faith traditions. Silent Unity takes prayer requests by phone at 800-NOW-PRAY as well as online at *www.silent unity.org*.

*****

Reflection Points

What role does prayer play in your life?

In what ways could prayer support you throughout the day at home, at work and in all your relationships?

The Peacebuilder Challenge

Think of a personal or global issue that has caused you concern. Call Silent Unity at 1-800-NOW-PRAY (1-800-669-7729) and experience the power of coming together for prayer in the name of peace. This is a free call.

11

REACHING OUT

James Trapp

Rev. James Trapp is the CEO of Unity Worldwide Ministries. He believes that Unity principles, such as honoring the divinity of all people, are relevant to select societal issues. Here he discusses the role of religion in the evolution to peace, and how each of us has the power to "reach out" to create a better world for all people.

> "Once we set the intention that we will be the peace-makers, that we will be the channels of peace, then we can transform any situation, regardless of what the appearances may be."
> —Rev. James Trapp, CEO of Unity Worldwide
> Ministries

Q: James, what does peace mean to you?

Peace, among other things, is a way of being. It is a state of consciousness. I believe it starts with us. We have to begin to feel as if we have the peace within ourselves, first and foremost.

But then I think you begin to expand that to people outside of yourself and out to your entire environment so that you're living in harmony. Often peace is really about how we move in alignment with those that we may consider to be different from ourselves.

I believe one thing that helps us get there is to move from a state of toleration to a state of acceptance, a state of full appreciation for another. Once you have that kind of relationship with another person—full appreciation of them—you no longer can see them as others. You no longer see them as objects, and you begin to realize that whatever energy you send out toward another individual, you also are keeping for yourself. So you want to send out the energy of peace. It's really a way of being, a way of relating, among other things.

Throughout history, religion has been one of the biggest instigators of violence in the world, and I think it causes people to become a bit tired of religion. How does something like religion, something that's intended to serve a person's spirit, end up creating pain and suffering?

Religion originally meant "to tie together, to bind together." What has happened over time is that some of our religious traditions have moved away from that basic understanding of what religion is about and have created more of a sense of separation: "Us versus them." "I am right and you are wrong."

It's that I-am-right-you-are-wrong consciousness that can lead to conflict. It will lead to labeling someone else as just an object, and can lead to violence against others. So there's a great deal of history that creates a sense of separation between the people in some religions, although that's not the original intent of most of the religions of the world.

What we have to do is go back to the basic reason that religion exists. It's to bind ourselves together and know that we're interconnected on a soul level, on a spiritual level. If we do that and we realize that, then how we act and think toward others will be entirely different than any kind of sense of separation that religion sometimes creates.

Q: *Tell us a little bit about Unity in terms of the Unity philosophy about religion. Is Unity a religion? Is it not? Is it interfaith?*

Unity is a way of life. Look at what I call *religiosity*, which Unity seeks not to be. Religiosity has more to do with doctrines, dogmas, rules and regulations. Unity really seeks to be in alignment with a spiritual way of being, and that means that who we are and how we act is more important than what we say we believe.

I believe it was Mahatma Gandhi who was asked what his religious message was. He responded to the reporter who thought Gandhi was going to give some sort of dissertation or exhortation on his spiritual principles. Instead he said, "My life is my message."

So as we say in Unity, your religion is who you are and how you act. It goes beyond a particular set of doctrines or dogmas, although we do believe in universal spiritual principles. But in the end, our life is our religion.

Q: *What is your vision for the role of organized religion in creating a peaceful world?*

I think it begins by breaking down any seeming barriers that we have created between people. I'm of the belief that all of the things of separation that lead to violence, sometimes in the name of religion, are all human-created. So we have to begin to go beyond the human ego and begin to look at ourselves as spiritual beings that are interconnected on that spiritual level, on that soul level. We want to rise above the human-made lines of separation, the human-made lines of demarcation, and understand that we are all in this together. How we act toward ourselves and how we act toward others impacts the collective.

What we want to do is go beyond the labels of any particular religion, find out where we meet with common ground as spiritual beings, and from that perspective, determine how we relate to one another. If we truly understand our spiritual nature, which is straight from the Spirit of God Itself, then we will act in a way that's in accord with peace, understanding, support and appreciation. I believe that's what religion is supposed to do, to bind us together on that more profound level as spiritual beings.

Q: *What does it mean to you to "reach in and reach out" as a means of establishing peace?*

It means if we're going to have peace on the planet, it starts with our spiritual intention. It begins by us having peace as our intention, then speaking in alignment with that intention, praying affirmatively so that our vibration and our way of being is in tune with that intention.

Then, of course, to carry out our actions in any way, shape or form that supports that intention in our interaction with others, with other communities, and ultimately between communities so that this will be the way of being for our world. That's one of the goals of prayer. We get clear on what it is that we want to be, then we do everything to make sure we anchor that idea into our lives and in our world.

Q: *Talk about what Unity as a movement is doing to express this theme of reaching in, reaching out and changing the world. What is Unity doing?*

Over the last couple of years or so, we began to look at what our purpose is as a collective movement, beyond just a goal or a mission. It is, as I like to say, the deepest river that we can dive into.

We set our own vision and purpose as a collective to be centered in God so that we can co-create a world that works for all. If we begin to have a world that works for all, then we know that we can have a world in which there is peace as the dominant way of being in our world. That's our intention. Of course, now we have to begin to bring that intention into some actual practices once we begin to make that part of our own prayer consciousness.

In Costa Rica, there is a fabulous program called *BePeace*, and it has been supported and endorsed by the highest elected officials in that country. *BePeace* equips people with tools, such as nonviolent communication and HeartMath, to help them become the peaceful agents we know we can be. They make that part of the curriculum in the schools there. So they're looking at being a model of possibilities. What does it take to be an ambassador of peace? We're looking at ways we can go even beyond that.

Q: *If you go to the Unity website, one of the things you'll find is a powerful declaration that states, "Unity stands for peace in our lifetime." What does that statement mean to you?*

It goes back to one of our basic principles: What we believe is ultimately what we will experience. Once we set the intention that we will be the peacemakers, that we will be the channels of peace, then we can transform any situation into a consciousness of peace in our lifetime and on the planet, regardless of what the appearances may be.

It's really just an outpicturing of the collective consciousness. As we change our individual consciousness—one mind, one awareness at a time—we then add that up to a collective consciousness of peace. Then our world begins to outpicture the very consciousness that we have. I believe that once we move in that direction, and as critical mass begins to hold that intention, we anchor the consciousness of peace in our world.

Q: *Rev. Lynne Brown led us in a prayer for reaching in for that inner state of peace. Would you be willing to lead us in a prayer for reaching out and bringing that peace to the world?*

I'd be more than happy to do that, Mindy.

Let us settle into this awareness of peace. We know that God is known by so many names, but among other things, God is known as Love, and God is peace. We, being made in the image and likeness of God, hold the same consciousness of peace, and once we make peace the activity of our awareness, it becomes our opportunity to anchor peace on the planet in our real experience through our actions.

I believe it was Rev. Dr. Martin Luther King who said—I paraphrase him—peace will not come on the wheels of inevitability. So we are reminded that for us to bring forth the peace that we know our hearts and minds long for, we must do our parts to bring forth peace.

We begin with ourselves, knowing that we can never have in our world that which we're not ready to become; and to be so, we become the peace that we want to see. Then through the words that we speak, we show our alignment with the qualities of peace.

All the actions that we take are actions that recognize that peace is indeed the way of being of God. It is the way of being of ourselves. It is the way of being for those that we interact with. We bring forth this peace through our actions by seeing and acting from the highest point of view toward others, recognizing that as we support another in any way, shape or form, then we begin to awaken to the connection that is always there on a spiritual level between us and everyone else.

We go forth every morning beginning to ask ourselves, "What is it that I can do today to anchor peace on Earth? What is it that I can speak today that brings the vibration of peace in my community and my world?"

As we begin to do that, not only do we transform ourselves, we begin to transform the very world in which we live through our thoughts, through our words, and through the actions that we take. We recognize that it's already done in the mind and heart of God, and our task is simply to rise up in consciousness to be one with what God has already done. Knowing that it is already there for us, we accept it gracefully and peacefully in the name and in the spirit of the living God. And so it is. Amen.

Q: *Amen. It is such a great joy to not only reach in, but also to reach out and to know what we are doing is making a difference. There're so many exciting projects happening right now in the Unity movement. Give us a taste of a few different ways people are expressing peace.*

You're right. There are a number of things.

Even the great think-tanks on the planet today have said there's no military solution to peace on the planet. It has to come from something far more than that. If we have a world where everyone is fed, and we have people with clean water and education, then we'll be moving toward really having peace on Earth and goodwill toward all.

For example, one of the Unity churches in Miami does an annual backpack drive that looks for poor communities that may be in their area or outside the country to fill a backpack with all the office and school supplies they will need for the year. We have other communities that have aligned with others, for example, in Africa, to help support the creation of wells for clean water.

Recently, our entire Unity movement partnered with an organization called *Soles4Souls* in which we provide shoes for individuals who don't have shoes. It could be an organization. It could be a country outside the United States. It could be a family. It could be a school.

One of our goals was to have more than 500,000 pairs of shoes distributed throughout the world. We often take for granted that shoes are just available to everyone, but they're not. When we provide these shoes to others, it helps alleviate diseases they may be experiencing. So we can begin to create more stability for others. Those are some of the things that we're doing in our movement and there are so many more of those taking place as well.

*****

Rev. James Trapp is president and CEO of Unity Worldwide Ministries (*www.unity.org*). Rev. James Trapp was ordained in 1994 and served as a dynamic presence at Unity on the Bay in Miami, Florida, for 10 years, growing a vibrant spiritual community that is racially, ethnically and culturally diverse. He supports the Unity movement in carrying out the great commission of spreading the good news and co-creating with spirit to transform lives and our world.

*****

Reflection Points:

Reflect upon the idea "My life is my message." What message are you currently sending the world through your example?

What message would you like to send to the world through your example?

The Peacebuilder Challenge:

Spend time in prayer, meditation or contemplation regarding the message you want your life to bring to the world. From this place within, identify one specific action you can take to "reach out" and live by example. Take one inspired action based on your intuitive wisdom.

12

THE POWER OF LOVE

Kute Blackson

Kute Blackson was born in Ghana, West Africa, as the child of a Japanese mother and a Ghanaian father. His multicultural upbringing prepared him to serve as a next-generation world leader out to awaken millions to the power of love and to living their inspired destiny. He shares with us his teachings on "Liberated Living," and how to live fully in the consciousness of Love.

"We're going through perhaps the greatest spiritual revolution that the world has ever seen. We're being forced to get in touch with what's truly important. We're being forced to let go of who we thought we were, and that's taking us to a deeper access of the true spirit of who we are, which is love."
—Kute Blackson, life coach and inspirational speaker

Q: *Kute, on your website it says that you came to the United States with two suitcases and a dream. What was the dream that you brought with you?*

From my very first memories as a young man about age 5, I always felt a deep calling to serve humanity, to have a positive impact, and to really spread a message of consciousness, spirituality and love. You could say the dream had me then.

I was supposed to take over my father's churches, and to cut a long story short, I was ordained at 14, and started reading hundreds and hundreds of books on personal development, meditation, spirituality and metaphysics.

The dream was really to come to America, and to go and find mentors—all the authors, teachers and mystics that I'd been reading about as a kid. I wanted to come find these folks, learn from them, study with them at their feet, so to speak, and go into that field to teach and inspire. That's the dream that pulled me.

I really believe that when you feel a calling, it is the Divine whispering to us. It's the universe's way of moving us forward. The means unfolded, so I showed up in America.

Q: *Sometimes that's the biggest step—just showing up. I think a lot of people right now are feeling that call and maybe not even knowing exactly what it's calling them toward. Do you experience this? How do you work with people to help them identify what that calling is?*

Deep within us is an Innate Intelligence. It's the Intelligence of Life that's living and breathing in us, and if we're willing to be still enough, it will whisper to us. It will speak to us. It will nudge us forward. Yet often our mind gets in the way and we question it.

We start getting into thinking about how we're going to do it, and before we've even acknowledged the impulse, we've negated it. The first step is to create time in our daily lives to be still enough to listen to the Impulse of Life that is seeking to be given birth through us. Rather than asking "How?" it's just taking the time to acknowledge the Impulse to say *Yes!* to It, and to begin taking action, leaning into It, and moving forward.

If we do that, we don't have to know what will be tomorrow. We don't have to know what will be next. If we're willing to just dive into the unknown and take one step, the next step will lead to the next step, which will lead to the next step. In the process of life itself, a deeper purpose will reveal itself.

It's so important, I think, as a first step on a practical level to take that daily time-out of the business of life to listen. We must listen to the Intelligence that is already inside of us because contained in us is all of life. All the information we've ever wanted to know is there just waiting for us to tune in to it.

Q: In your programs, you talk about "liberated living." Tell us what "liberated living" means to you.

Liberated living is, simply put, just being in touch with the true essence of who we are. So often we're conditioned in our personality. We're conditioned by television, media, radio, society and culture. We get identified with our body and we get identified with our story.

For me, liberated living is stepping outside of who we think we are, questioning who we truly are, getting in touch with the true source of who we are and living that fully in the world in a way that's aligned with our deepest truth. It's about living freely beyond condition, beyond the past.

When you take away all of these identifications that you might think you are, you start finding out what's really there. You start finding out who you really are. To me, that's living liberated. It's living freely. It's living in touch with the source.

Q: What is your vision? Imagine a world where the masses are living liberated lives. What does the world look like?

Love is flowing. We're not buying into the illusion of color, race or separation.

We're living in a culture where love is flowing, where we're loving radically, where we're truly in touch with who we are and what's real, and there's cooperation, harmony, unity and peace.

To me, peace and unity arise when we're in touch with the recognition of who we are, and from that place, we recognize ultimately at the deepest level that we are one; from that place, love flows. We are being called to love, especially as we go through some intense times right now.

Some people are calling it a crisis. I say it's an opportunity. I feel like we're going through perhaps the greatest spiritual revolution that the world has ever seen as structures collapse, ideas collapse, and people are losing things that they thought were important. We're being forced to get in touch with what's truly important.

We're being forced to let go of who we thought we were and who we may have identified ourselves to be, and I think that's taking us to a deeper access of the true spirit of who we are, and who each and everyone of us is. To me, that's bringing us closer, and I think reconnecting us to what's important, which is love and loving.

Q: *I agree. This is such a critical time in history, and such an exciting time because there is so much that could be born from where we are. From where we stand as an individual in this world and this moment, with all the things going on, what is our choice regarding peace? Where are we in terms of choosing our destiny right now?*

You could say we are participating in this whole grand evolutionary process that's happening. We are front and center in this process, and we do have the choice that no matter what is going on in our world, we can love. We can accept what's happening, accept everything that's happening in the world and truly, even in the midst of that, dare to love. I feel that's what we're being called to do, to dare to reach out, dare to love, dare to remember who we really are.

We live in a culture where we worship superheroes that fly, athletes that jump, firewalkers and skydivers, but to me the great boldness and courage, especially in these times, lie in those that are willing to reach out, open their hearts and love. I feel that these are the new heroes of this generation, and they are you and me.

We'll always have reason, but we cannot live in fear. If we live in fear, we're just prisoners of our own mind. So we have a choice: We can either live in fear or we can live boldly. I feel we're being called forth.

In the past, maybe you needed to go to India or go to a meditation training in the Himalayas somewhere, but life has come to us, and I feel like the world itself is the yoga studio. The opportunity for our spiritual practice is moment to moment to moment. There is opportunity in each moment of our lives.

Q: Talk about your personal practices. As you move through your day, what are the things that keep you grounded in the consciousness of peace?

I've done hundreds and hundreds of different practices. I'll be honest, Mindy, on some level, it has become simpler. The question I ask myself as a practical practice is "Am I loving or am I not, right now?"

It's great to read the books. It's great to meditate. It's great to raise kundalini. It's great to go to church. It's great to pray. It's great to do yoga. It's great to do all of those things. But the question I dare to ask myself and others as a daily embodied practice is "Am I loving right now or am I not?"

The fear is great, but am I living what Christ talked about, the compassionate Buddha talked about, the compassionate Mother Teresa—am I living it? For me, that's become a simple way to practice this: "Am I loving or am I not?" and really feeling that and daring to just stretch myself in that domain.

Q: Peacebuilding is really not about fixing or settling conflict. It's about creating a world of love. So what is the role of the individual, and then what is our role as a collective in terms of creating this vision?

The first place where we must start is within ourselves, because the world is simply a reflection of our own consciousness. The world right now is a reflection of the collective consciousness of each and every one of us put together.

We may not be able to bring peace in the Middle East, Afghanistan or Darfur, but what we can do is begin with ourselves, begin in our own heart to look in ourselves and look at where the war is going on inside ourselves.

Where am I not accepting myself? How am I not loving myself? Where am I not forgiving myself? Where am I dropping bombs of judgment in my own self about my past, about who I should be, what I should be, what I could be doing? Have a moment of grace, a moment of compassion, and bring loving, tenderness and kindness to yourself.

The first step is to look inside and bring compassion and tenderness to ourselves so we can come into a place of acceptance of who we are and what we are as we continue to grow. From that place, I feel we can then move out into the world and maybe bring peace.

But it has to start with ourselves. When we are being peace, we will radiate an energy and a vibration that will then start affecting our spouses, our children, our community or those around us, and that will then start having another layer of effect. That level will affect the next level, and it will ripple out. I feel the part we are in control of is working with ourselves, and bringing that acceptance to ourselves.

Q: I love how you mention the bombs of judgment, the war that we wage within ourselves. I think many of us do that, and we've done it so long, it's completely unconscious. We wouldn't even recognize that there is a war within us. What becomes possible through that awareness and inner transformation?

Yes, I think awareness is the first step, and probably the most important step. If you're not aware, there is no possibility for a shift. In the moment of awareness, the next thing one can do is begin questioning.

Begin questioning the judgment. Start by questioning ourselves. Begin looking at the judgment and actually seeing through the illusion of the judgment. Then from that place, bring a moment of compassion, a moment of tenderness, a moment of self-forgiveness. That will create a new energy within us. That will create a new space within us, a new ability to breathe and a new opening for grace.

We can be at peace with ourselves as we are. That's when grace and love blossoms, and from that place, we're not just talking about peace, we're actually *being* peace. We are *being* at peace with what is, *being* at peace with who we are. We're actually embodying and being peace itself. To me, that's where transformation happens.

Gandhi said to be the change that you're seeking to have happen. So I feel like it's time that we step up, be the peace and embody the peace, because everything is infinitely interconnected. I've heard it said that a butterfly flapping its wings on one side of the world can create a storm or similar ecological effect on the other side of the planet.

So by moving into a state of peace, of self-loving, of self-compassion, of just self-acceptance of all of who we are, the light and the dark, we'll move into a resonance of peace, of the embodiment of peace. We will be peace, and that is powerful.

Q: How do we know when we're there? Or how do we know when at least we're on track?

I think we will feel equanimity. We will feel calmness. Life won't be perfect. There will be ups and there will be downs. There will be rain and there will be sun. There will be light and there will be dark. The whole gamut of the relative existence of life will still be there, but we won't be resisting it, judging it or fighting it. We'll just be with it and from that place, there'll be space. From that place, there will be calmness. There will be peace. There will be more neutrality, less reactivity and more space to be with what's happening as it's happening, and just love what's happening. To me, peace is not the absence of conflict. It's just being in graceful relationship with what is.

*****

Kute Blackson (*www.kuteblackson.com*) is known for his high energy, his cutting-edge ideas, his dynamic and life-changing presentations. Known nationally as "The Transformation Coach," Kute is a certified hypnotherapist and NLP practitioner, assisting individuals and corporations in creating authentic change. He is also a radio talk-show personality, having had his own radio show called *Beyond Boundaries* on KYPA in Los Angeles. As founder and president of The Blackson Group, Kute is a dynamic life coach and inspirational speaker.

*****

Reflection Points

How would *you* answer Kute's questions: Where am I not accepting myself? How am I not loving myself? Where am I dropping bombs of judgment in my own self about my past, about who I should be, what I should be, what I could be doing?

Kute emphasized the importance of listening to and acknowledging the "Impulse of Life." What do you feel Life is seeking to bring forth through you?

The Peacebuilder Challenge

Gift yourself with "a moment of grace." Indulge in an action that demonstrates love, tenderness and kindness to yourself.

13

BULLETPROOF FORGIVENESS

Azim Khamisa

For many people, the most difficult step on the path to peace is the one called forgiveness. How can we forgive the unforgivable? To answer this question, we talked with Azim Khamisa, a man who knows what it means to forgive. Azim lost his only son to a senseless gang-related murder. Today he has not only forgiven his son's killer, he is teaching other people how to find the bulletproof spirit that leads to true peace as the founder of the Tariq Khamisa Foundation.

> "When we produce leaders that understand forgiveness instead of revenge, and understand that from conflict, you can create love and unity, then hopefully, we have a shot at world peace."
> —Azim Khamisa, founder of the Tariq Khamisa
> Foundation

Q: *Azim, tell us about your son and what happened on that tragic day so many years ago.*

It was 14 years ago, although it seems like yesterday. My son Tariq was a student at San Diego State University, and worked on Fridays and Saturdays for a local Italian restaurant. The area was middle class and he delivered pizzas there all the time. But on this particular evening, he was lured out by a youth gang.

He knocked on several apartments in that building and found out nobody had ordered a pizza. So he came back to the car, put the pizzas in the trunk, and as he was about to leave the scene of the crime, he was accosted by four youth gang members. Two of them were 14, and the leader of the gang was 18.

The leader handed a nine-millimeter gun to one of the 14-year-olds as my son was trying to back away from the driveway, and gave the order, "Bust him, Bones."

Bones was the kid's gang nickname and he fired one round, which entered my son's body under the left armpit. It traveled across the upper part of his chest and actually exited on the right armpit.

As the coroner told me afterwards, "It was a perfect path." I said to him, "A perfect path?" He said, "Yes, we don't often see a path like this." He meant that it was perfect in the sense that it destroyed all the vital organs, and my son died a couple of minutes later, drowning in his own blood at the age of 20 over a lousy pizza.

Q: It's difficult to even imagine what you must have experienced as a parent.

Yes, it brought my life to a crashing halt, as you can imagine. I don't know what is more complicated in life than losing a child. It's the worst nightmare of any parent.

Q: What was your journey? I imagine the first response would probably be rage, anger.

Not really. First, it was pain. It felt like a nuclear bomb had gone off in my heart. I've never experienced pain like that. It was so painful that I couldn't be in my body, and I had my first out-of-body experience. I left my body.

I remember life draining out of me from my head to my toes, and I believe I went into the loving arms of God. He held me in an embrace for a long time, and when the explosion subsided, He sent me back to my body with the wisdom that there are victims at both ends of the gun.

I don't have family. I live by myself in San Diego, and my best friend and his wife were with me an hour and a half after I found out. The first thing my buddy said to me was, "Whoever these kids are, I hope they fry in hell."

I looked at him and said, "I don't feel that way. I see that there are victims at both ends of the gun."

I remember him breaking down and crying as he said, "Where do you get this strength? If somebody took my son, I would not only want the killer. I would want the whole clan."

So my journey started at that level, because while I had compassion for my son, I also felt empathy and compassion for the kid that killed him. If I had any anger, it was more aimed at society, because so many of our kids join gangs for the wrong reasons. I don't believe we are doing enough to stop that.

Q: *Tell us what you have done because you took another step.*

The first few months were just terrible. You don't eat. You don't sleep. Your biological functions change. I was suicidal at one point. I did not know how to live without my son. He was an important part of my family.

But eventually, I survived and I looked into gangs because I did not know much about youth gangs. I used to work in the international investment banking field, and I still do some of that, but not a lot. I was really living in a different world. I traveled the world.

Then I couldn't get out of bed. I thought, Where did this energy go? I wanted to learn more about why kids join gangs, and I found out that the reasons they join gangs were horrific.

I was told they joined gangs because they get respect—gang members are actually respected by their peers—or they join gangs because they live in areas where if they don't join this gang, they're targeted by a rival gang. There are a lot of racial gangs—Hispanic, African-American, Asian, white gangs—so they join to get a sense of belonging, or they join because it's expected of them.

I've met gang members now that are five generations deep and I thought, Wait a minute: We are the United States of America. We are the richest nation in the world. We're the only superpower. What are we doing with kids that are joining gangs for the wrong reasons?

So nine months after Tariq died, I created the Tariq Khamisa Foundation, which is named after him to help my family and me deal with the loss in a meaningful way. It's online at *www.tkf.org*, and the mission statement of the foundation is to stop kids from killing kids by breaking the cycle of youth violence. We do this by 1) saving lives, 2) empowering their right choices, 3) teaching the principles of peacemaking, nonviolence and forgiveness.

I reached out to the guardian and grandfather of my son's killer soon after I established the foundation, and I told him, "I come to you not in anger, resentment or retribution, because what I see here is that we both lost a child. My child died. Your child, you lost to the adult prison system. There's nothing I can do to get my child back from the dead and there's nothing you can do to get your grandson out of prison, but the one thing that we can do is we can stop others from making the same mistake that your grandson did. I've come to ask for your help. I have this foundation. I have a lofty mission statement. Will you help me? Will you work with me so we can go out to the community and make sure that we bring this message to kids: "Don't join gangs for the wrong reason"?

That was 14 years ago, and when we fast-forward to today, the foundation has been amazingly successful. I've personally spoken to 500,000 kids. We've reached 8 million kids via broadcast into the classrooms.

We are school-based and we are teaching the principles of peacemaking, of nonviolence, and of forgiveness. We are successfully keeping kids away from gangs, guns and violence, and have substantially reduced violence on campus. We have won some 60 awards. I've written three books. It's changed my life, and now 80 percent of my time is spent in talking to kids and doing this work.

Q: *What does peace mean to you?*

I think peace is an attitude. When I think about Tony, the kid who killed my son, my blood pressure does not go up. He has a safe passage through my mind.

I think true forgiveness can get you to peace. I believe that many of us are either skin bags of resentment against people that have hurt us or we are in guilt of things we have done to other people. I think that you can't achieve a state of peace until you are able to forgive, so I think forgiveness is a very important part of this whole journey.

Now there're obviously two different types of forgiveness. One is forgiving somebody who's hurt you and the other one is forgiving yourself for the hurt you've caused. I teach a course on both of these and if you like, I can explain to you the process that I teach.

Q: *Yes. Let's take an example. Let's say there's someone who has experienced something that, to them, feels or seems unforgivable. What would you recommend as a process for them?*

First of all, you need to understand forgiveness. Forgiveness is not about judgment. Very often, we think, How can you forgive somebody who murdered your son?

I tell people, "It's not that I forgive Tony for murdering my son. What he did was very wrong, but the reason I forgave is because I didn't want to go through life as a victim. I didn't want to go through life on crutches and say, "I've lost my one and only son."

I said, "I had a very full life when my son was alive. I traveled the globe, made good money, and had a good life. Then I didn't have a life and I know that there's no quality being a victim."

I forgave so I would stop being a victim. Unless you forgive, you remain a victim; and if you remain a victim, there's no quality of life. I did it for me. It is a selfish act when you think about it. Why would you want such important real estate of your psyche occupied by somebody who's hurt you? Why not free that real estate in your psyche so love and joy can live there?

That's the purpose of forgiveness. You're doing it for you. In terms of how you do it, I teach three basic milestones.

The first one is to acknowledge that you have been wronged. This is the painful piece. As a culture, we don't like pain. Pain is not a bad thing, because it molds you into a better person if you can use the pain in a productive manner. For the slightest headache, you go get an extra-strength Tylenol. Then you go take another one four hours later, or you take a Prozac prescription if you're depressed. It doesn't sustain you. So I teach how to get through the pain, and you do that through ritual.

I like to journal. I walk miles on the beach. I meditate two hours a day. I used to meditate an hour a day. I read inspirational literature. I practice as a Sufi Muslim, and we have a lot of rituals that help us deal with the loss of a child or family member.

The main thing I teach in this particular step or milestone is that you have to go through the pain, but you also have to have a sunset on that pain because if you don't, then you remain a victim.

The second milestone is about understanding that you have to give up all the resulting resentment. Mandela didn't write this quote, but he made it famous: "Resentment is like drinking poison and waiting for your enemy to die."

Q: Yes, it doesn't work that way.

Right. If you stay in resentment, who are you hurting? You're hurting yourself, right?

To me, that's self-abuse. You might as well take a whip and beat yourself up. You get through resentment with intention and empathy. I teach in my workshops how you get that intention out there through the process of meditation, and how you develop empathy. The process to forgiveness starts with that empathy. From empathy, you get to compassion. From compassion, you get to forgiveness. Unless you have empathy, you won't get to compassion, and unless you get to compassion, you can't get to forgiveness.

The last part of the milestone in forgiving others is to reach out to the offender. Reach out to the offender with love and compassion. Not every one of us has to reach out to the murderer of our child. Very often, the issues are father-son, mother-daughter, ex-husband-ex-wife. I do this work in the business world as well with business partners.

We reach out and understand that as humans, we are fallible. Through that reaching out, you can create a deeper bond. It's exactly what happened in the journey that the grandfather and I have been on together for 14 years.

He and I are now like brothers. There's so much love we have for each other. He's an important part of my life and I would never have met him had his grandson not taken the life of my son. So in conflict and in crisis, opportunity exists.

Q: *Yes. So what is your relationship now with Tony?*

I met him five years after the tragedy. I met his grandfather nine months after, but it took me a long time to muster enough courage to go see Tony, although I did know at some point I had to do that to complete my own journey of forgiveness. I'm very pleased that I did do that.

Not only did I forgive him when I met him. I remember looking in his eyes for a very long time thinking I wanted to find a murderer in him. But I didn't. What I saw in him was another soul much like mine, much like any other soul. Sure, he had done something very wrong, but I was able to climb into his eyes, climb down to his soul and feel his humanity.

I realized that this is a young man who made a big mistake, but just because he made a big mistake does not make him inhuman.

We have a good relationship. I told him, "Tony, when you come out, you'll have a job waiting for you at the foundation." I'm actually working at trying to get him out early because he's not due to come out until 2017.

He's changed as a result of me giving him an offer of a job. He's shifted his life. He's passed his GED. He's doing college courses. He's studying very hard. This kid used to hate to read, by the way. He reads five books a month now.

We write to each other. I don't visit him as often because he's far away, but we write to each other all the time. There's a lot of love that I've created for him in the foundation. He participates. We're able to get him on camera. We have two and a half hours of him on camera that we use in the program in schools. He understands what we're doing and I look forward to the day when he can join us.

Q: What is your vision for what you are building through your foundation as it relates to world peace?

We have a message that teaches through our story.

The first message is that violence is real and hurts everyone. People have a different impression of violence because they see a lot of violence on television, and then they see the people who are the victims and perpetrators out on a boat sipping on a cocktail.

We tell them, "That's not real. What's real is there are family members of victims and perpetrators that suffer and suffer and suffer." They see the pain on my face, they see the pain on the grandfather's face, and they say, "This is real." So our first key message is that violence is real and hurts everyone.

Our second key message is that actions have consequences. Tony won't be out until he's 46 years old, and he went into prison at 14. He will not go out on a date, to movies or a game. It's important when you're a teenager. I say to young people, "Think about that. He'll be 46 before he comes out."

Number three: We can all make good and nonviolent choices. It's a choice. If you meet violence with violence, then the pain will never go away. You can't destroy dark with dark. If you go into a dark room and turn the light on, you can destroy the dark. And you can destroy violence with nonviolence, so we can all make good and nonviolent choices.

Our fourth message is that you can offer forgiveness instead of revenge, because revenge is a precursor of every new act of violence. Forgiveness is a better way to go because it healed me. It healed my family. It healed Tony. It healed his family. They see that.

Our fifth key message is that everyone, including you, deserves to be treated well. We live in a multicultural society. You go into the schools and it's like a rainbow of human color. Kids will tease and I tell them, "It doesn't matter." I said, "I'm a Muslim. Tony's grandfather is Christian. He's African American. I am Eastern. But we are brothers. So everyone—it doesn't matter what they look like—needs to be treated well."

Our last key message is that from conflict, you can create love and unity. That's one of my favorites because if every conflict in the world could be resolved like ours, we would have world peace.

My personal vision is to teach these six key messages to every classroom in the world. It may not happen in my lifetime, but at least I've set the stage to say that through our story. We teach the six key messages in a very powerful way and we are very good at doing it.

Hopefully, someday we'll be in every classroom in the world. We'll produce leaders that understand forgiveness instead of revenge, and understand that from conflict, you can create love and unity. Hopefully, we have a shot at world peace.

*****

Hailed by dignitaries such as the Dalai Lama, former President Bill Clinton and Vice President Al Gore, **Azim Khamisa** (*www.azimkhamisa.com*) carries his inspirational message of forgiveness, peace and hope into a world in desperate need of each. Azim is the author of *The Secrets of the Bulletproof Spirit: How to Bounce Back From Life's Hardest Hits*. His foundation, The Tariq Khamisa Foundation (*www.tkf.org*), services roughly 3,000 students annually. The work of the Foundation continues to change the lives of young people by empowering them to make positive and nonviolent choices.

*****

Reflection Points

Think of people who have wronged you in the past. Have you allowed yourself to feel and acknowledge the injustice?

Are you willing to let go of any resulting resentment? What do you need to do to allow yourself to let go?

The Peacebuilder Challenge

Reach out to your offenders with love and compassion.

14

SACRED ACTIVISM

Andrew Harvey

An internationally acclaimed poet, novelist, translator, mystical scholar and spiritual teacher, Andrew Harvey has published more than 20 books including The Hope: A Guide to Sacred Activism. *The founder of the Institute for Sacred Activism, Andrew joins us to issue the call to spiritually motivated social action, and to share a vision of a grassroots network of change agents.*

> "We have to start descending into the reality of our situation armed with the love of God, with the wisdom of God, with the passion of God and with the compassion of God."
>
> —Andrew Harvey, founder of the Institute
> for Sacred Activism

Q: *Andrew, what is a "sacred activist"?*

Mindy, what's going on in the world now really demands that everybody wakes up. We're in a dramatic and potentially extremely destructive, even terminal crisis that we need to respond to from the depths of ourselves, because time is running out. I've known this for a long time and I've meditated deeply on the force that could birth a new human race and reality—a new kind of human being who would be humble and co-creative with God of the new world. This force is, I believe, *sacred activism.*

The highest definition of *sacred activism* for me is that it is a third fire made when you unite the two most noble and sacred fires of the human soul: the passion for God with the passion for justice; the passion for God of the mystic with the passion for justice of the activist. What you get when you unite these fires is the fire of love and action, and this is a fire of dynamic passion, compassion and action that is blessed directly by the Divine, and has great intelligence and great wisdom of unity with all beings, all systems and with the will of God itself. This third fire can change the world.

Q: What does the call to sacred activism look like and feel like?

I think it works through heartbreak. All of us at this moment are aware that a major, major crisis is going on, and however much we all play the game of denial, there are things in the world which really, really break our hearts.

I have a friend whose heart is broken by the plight of the AIDS babies in the Congo and who is doing something to help that. I have another friend who has been heartbroken by what is happening to villages in Ecuador, and has gone out to help those villagers. I have friends who are so distressed at the way which people in this country have to scramble for necessary health supplies that they have set up free clinics. I have friends, in other words, who allow their hearts to be broken open by the real world and then follow that heartbreak not into paralysis and hysteria, but into a real act of compassion.

There are millions of people waiting to wake up in this way, and afraid to wake up to what's going on and afraid to feel the depths of what's going on. But when you do, when you let your heart break, what you'll find is it will be more heartbroken for one cause than others. You'll have a special cause at the very core of your heartbreak.

Mine is animals. I'm heartbroken about many things, but what really breaks my heart the most is the terrible, terrible suffering we've inflicted on animals on every level, and the great extinctions that we're carrying out through our greed and through our madness. I have devoted my voice to the rights of animals. This is how I put it in practice in my own life.

It takes a lot of courage to open to what's happening. It takes even greater courage to feel what's happening. But if you do so, confident that you'll be supported by the Divine Beloved, you'll be united to the Divine Presence ever more deeply when you let yourself feel the fullness of what's happening at this moment. When you do, you are initiated into this third fire, and you become a humble, creative and passionate servant of the great birth that's trying to take place in the middle of this chaos. There is a great death taking place.

Q: You write about that in your book. Let's talk first about the goal of sacred activism.

The goal of sacred activism is to save the planet. The goal of sacred activism is to mobilize the hearts of millions and millions of people, and then help them see the essence of this third fire and feel it.

The goal is to do two things: plunge into serious spiritual practice to be guided by the Divine and plunge into sacred, righteous and compassionate action in every realm of the world to save the situation. Without having a deep spiritual practice and spiritual knowledge, and without being in the throes of a great spiritual transformation, a person may take action but it will not be wise enough, will not be blessed enough, will not be powerful enough and will not allow enough of the divine force of the divine blessing to come through.

This is why for this time, what we're all being asked to do is to fuse together the opposites, fuse together masculine and feminine, heaven and earth, body and soul, and sacred practice and radical action. When we do fuse these opposites together, a holy new kind of human being is created. This represents a kind of evolution because what is created when all of these opposites are fused together is an embodied human divine being, someone who is in her body, in her illumined mind, in her heart aflame with passionate compassion for reality and in her body which is increasingly supple to the divine energies. It's this new kind of human being that sacred activism as the evolutionary force of divine love and action is destined to birth.

This is what I believe, and this is why I've written this book at this time; to help people see what is required. And what is required is that all of us wake up and accept that we have created a death machine that is in the process of destroying the planet, that we are all colluding with this death machine because all of us have shadows that are partly comforted by this death machine and partly rewarded by this death machine, and we have to start descending into the reality of the situation armed with the love of God, with the wisdom of God, with the passion of God and with the compassion of God.

We need to find the courage to bring the divine light down into our whole being and into our actions, because it's only the wisdom, the compassion and the passion for compassion of the divine light that is going to be able to help us through this next transition, which is going to be horrific and chaotic, but is actually a birth transition, which we will survive if we love enough.

Q: Everything that you're saying here is the recipe for stepping into the evolution of peace that's happening. What do you believe is "peace on earth"?

The deepest thing that peace means to me is respect, and one of the concepts that I love most from my study of Sufi mysticism is a word called *adab*. Adab means "total courtesy of soul towards another being."

For me, peace begins with a transformation of the soul and with the revelation that all other beings on this planet are as divine as you are. They're all created from the divine light. All beings from the flea to the whale are manifestations of the glory of God and they are all literally brimming over with divine presence when you see with the eyes of the awakened mystic.

Inevitably, from that understanding flows tremendous love, tremendous compassion, and tremendous hunger to see all things cherished and protected. This great desire is the foundation of all true peace. It's awakening this desire in the human heart to see all human beings well, whatever their color, whatever their religion, and whatever their sexuality, simply because they are all as divine as you; to see all animals protected because they are voiceless and unprotected creatures of the divine mother; and to really love the world with the sacred *adab* that it deserves.

Q: I agree. You're talking about bringing together the best of activism with the best of spiritual practice.

The mystics will go on praying while the last forest burns down and the activist will continue to be in divided consciousness if they go on being fuelled by rage, anger, blame and division. So the mystics have a narcissism that is the addiction to transcendence and that, I think, afflicts all mystics to some extent. The activists have a form of narcissism that is an addiction to doing, an addiction to achieving and an addiction to a messiah complex. All of these shadows are now very obvious both in the spiritual world and in the activist world.

But the wonderful truth is that if you fuse the wisdom of the mystic with the wisdom of the activist, the wisdom of the activist cures the mystic's addiction to not doing anything, and the wisdom of the mystic cures the activist's addiction to doing for its own sake. So you have the possibility in this marriage of opposites, which creates a new kind of being, the healing of the shadows that have afflicted both kinds of approaches.

This is very, very hopeful. It's difficult to do because it really challenges the mystic to get real about the agony of the world and it really challenges the activist to do the inner work before giving themselves the right to tell everybody else how to do the outer work. Those kinds of beings are going to be very challenged by this, but if they accept the challenge and go through what they need to go through, they'll find that they have much greater levels of peace, passion and power available to them, and a much greater authority in the world.

Q: One of the things you talk about in your book The Hope *is the idea of "Networks of Grace."*

A "Network of Grace" is a group of six to 12 people in a local community who meet together as sacred activists to pray together, to support each other, and to set real goals that they hold each other to. Networks of Grace, I've suggested, should be built around real passions to do real things in the real world.

Say you discover that you're heartbroken for animals. Then establish a Network of Grace for those in your local community who want to work with animals. Pray with them and help them realize a real project in your community.

What Networks of Grace really do is create *imaginal* cells. Imaginal cells are the things that wake up in the gunge of a caterpillar's decaying body in the cocoon. Those imaginal cells constellate together and actually form the body of the butterfly that is going to break through the cocoon.

I see the spread of Networks of Grace, these cells built around prayer, deep love of each other and celebration of the possibilities of sacred activism, and the possibilities of true cooperation. I see these cells spreading like wildfire and having an enormous, emboldening effect on millions of people.

The clue to this transformation, this great birth, is the mobilization of us, the people—you and I who feel so desperately and deeply for the world, and you and I who long so desperately and so deeply to do something real to save our lives from paralysis, corruption and meaninglessness.

It's time to mobilize peacefully on a very big scale for the divine birth. Networks of Grace is, I'm convinced, one of the major ways of doing this. This is what I've been devoting myself to establishing.

*****

Andrew Harvey (*www.andrewharvey.net*) was born in south India in 1952 where he lived until he was 9 years old. It is this early period that he credits with shaping his sense of the inner unity of all religions and providing him with a permanent and inspiring vision of a world infused with the sacred. Andrew Harvey is founder/director of the Institute of Sacred Activism. He has a spiritual counseling practice in Chicago and is available for spiritual direction via phone.

*****

Reflection Points

What are the issues you see that break your heart?

What would be the one issue that most deeply touches your soul?

The Peacebuilder Challenge

Connect with others in your community to create a "Network of Grace." Gather to discuss a project you could prayerfully coordinate together to address the issue that pulls most at your heart.

15

THE PEACE DIET

John Raatz

John Raatz is the founder of the Global Alliance for Transformational Entertainment (GATE), an evolving membership community of creative, business and technical professionals in entertainment and the media, and others who realize the vital and expanding role the media and entertainment play in creating our lives, and who aspire to consciously transform that process for the benefit of all. He speaks with us about the possibility of a transformed entertainment industry and the impact of the media in the pursuit of a more peace-filled world.

> "I believe that our media diets, that which we consume in the form of media and entertainment, radically affect the states of our mental and emotional situation."
> —John Raatz, founder of the Global Alliance for Transformational Entertainment

Q: John, as you know, this series of interviews is focused on how we can facilitate the emergence of a more peaceful world. You are truly doing that, making huge waves in the world through your vision of transforming the entertainment industry. What do you see as the connection between media and entertainment, and our evolution to a more peaceful society?

There's an old adage that says, "Whatever you give attention to grows stronger in your life," and I think that most of us have media diets that do not give us peaceful nutrition.

We experience so many images, so many sounds, so many of the sensual aspects of war and violence through film, through television programming, through news shows, through newspapers and magazines. It's no wonder we live in a world that is filled with as much violence as it is when our media diet is comprised of so many such images.

I'm not advocating, by the way, that we completely eliminate those kinds of images when they're a part of a storyline, for example, in a movie or a TV show, but I am suggesting that we need a new set of values.

Another adage that I like is, "A new seed will yield a new crop." I believe that we need new media values for a new world. That's one of the purposes of transformational entertainment in media.

Q: I think a lot of people believe the answer is just to turn it off, and yet we don't want to turn it off. We love our media. We love entertainment. What you're doing is really innovative because you're not saying, "Turn it off." You're saying, "Let's just transform the message." What has the response been like so far?

The response has been phenomenal. It was actually more than I had expected, and I expected quite a bit. But the response worldwide has shown me that this is an idea whose time has come, and I'm not the only one promoting this kind of an idea, either. There are many, many people worldwide who believe that entertainment and media is a powerful force in our daily lives, and can assist us in the shift and the transformation.

Q: *What is your vision for what that would look like — a transformed entertainment industry?*

I'm not sure I can answer that question. I think it's very much in the state of process, in the state of development. I do believe we can have more balance. There's an audience of people out there who are starved for programming that uplifts us, that inspires us, that shares the wisdom of the world with us. I think, for starters, if we had more programming that reflected those kinds of values and preferences that we would be much, much better off.

Q: *Do you think the entertainment industry has a responsibility in creating this shift that's happening on our planet right now?*

I do. I think they have a responsibility for having contributed to it in its current condition, and I think they have a responsibility to help turn it around. It isn't just for profits. I have nothing against the entertainment companies making a profit. I hope they do make a profit. I just hope that their executives and others in seats of power can open to the idea, the possibility, the reality that there are lots of people out there who want something more. They want media and entertainment that reflect who we have become and who we are becoming, with more holistic, humanistic values.

Q: *The inaugural event for GATE was a huge success. Celebrities like Jim Carrey, Melissa Etheridge and Eckhart Tolle were all there taking part in the event. What do you think is the significance and the importance of bringing people together?*

There are three reasons: education, collaboration and advocacy.

We want to provide education to people who associate with GATE—an inner education. We want to provide them with resources that will deepen their connection to the consciousness of the essence that they are. We also want to help provide education in the form of mentorship to those people out there who are up-and-coming screenwriters, musicians, actors and actresses, or producers and directors.

We want to provide knowledge to them that will help them better navigate the entertainment business. In terms of connection and collaboration, we want to hold events so when people attend, they see that their peers and their colleagues are interested in the same kinds of things that they are.

We want to then encourage them to collaborate and share resources, share contacts, share money, and share projects. We basically want to collaborate to help bring forward entertainment media projects that reflect these humanistic values.

The third thing is advocacy. We would like the entertainment trade, as well as the general public, to become comfortable with the word *transformation*. In terms of genres of films, for example, you say there's "comedy," there's "action-adventure," there's "drama." We want you to say there's "transformation," so it becomes more and more acceptable as a genre.

Q: You talked about inner education. What do you think is the balance between the inner work and the outer manifestation?

My personal belief is that when a person's relationship with the consciousness of the essence that they are becomes more pronounced, that relationship naturally asserts itself in the work. It becomes integrated into the work. So if you're a director, a producer, a musician, a poet, a fine artist, a dancer or any number of other people who express art, that consciousness will pervade your work.

We feel that by providing people with resources to help deepen that connection, the integration of it into their daily lives and their work will become more and more pronounced.

Q: There are celebrities that are jumping onboard. What resistance is there to putting a name, a celebrity name out there in association with something so tied to spirituality and transformation?

Of course, there is resistance. But it really depends on where someone happens to be at a given time in their lives. There are people who are very well-known who are ready to stand on a roof of a building and shout out what their personal beliefs are in this arena, and then there are other people who prefer to be more silent about it but still do the work behind the scenes.

There will be people who come forward and express various issues. Jim Carrey has spoken publicly more and more about his own spirituality. He has spoken more and more about his interests in deep ecology and the environment. He has projects through his foundation in Madagascar, for example, that are designed to help the people of Madagascar become economically and ecologically sustainable. That's one example.

There are many, many actors, actresses, producers, directors, writers, musicians, studio executives, agents, managers, attorneys all in the entertainment media businesses who feel transformation in their own lives and who want to assist others to achieve the same.

Q: I strongly believe you are bringing people together in a way that really can have a profound impact on our world. What does peace mean to you?

A lot of people may feel that peace means an absence of conflict.

Personally, when I think of peace, I immediately think of inner peace. I think of wholeness. I think of totality. I mean that in the abstract, spiritual sense. I mean that in terms of consciousness itself. For me, peace means a connection with the innermost aspect of who I am. I know that to be consciousness.

I remember a teacher I once studied with who said that the individual is the basis of world peace. You can't legislate peace. It is something that comes from a collective of peaceful individuals. I strongly believe that.

I believe that our media diets, that which we metabolize in the form of media and entertainment, radically affects the states of our mental and emotional situation. When we expose our minds and our emotions to the peace within, if you will, it has a dramatic effect on how we relate to ourselves, to those closest to us, and to people in general.

Q: What do you see as the primary motivator for people doing that inner work on an individual level?

You know, I've tossed that question around a lot over the last several months and I've not come up with an answer. I'm not sure there is an answer. I think it has to do with the fact that everybody starts the journey of seeking in their own time. I bet if we asked a hundred different people what is it that prompted them to begin that search, they would all have a different answer.

I think it's something that just happens in everyone's life at one time or another. It could be prompted by an illness. It could be prompted by some sort of an inner realization in terms of one of the big questions in life. There's probably any number of things that actually prompts that search. These days, more and more, I prefer not to think too strictly about anything and think that I have an answer. I like staying in that field of openness and possibility because I think there's always more than one answer.

I love what Fred Alan Wolf says: "Don't be in the know. Be in the mystery. Stay in that state of openness to all possibilities."

Q: What would your vision be for how you and the work that you're doing could facilitate the shift that is happening on the planet?

I feel that the boundaries between work and play have long ago dissolved. It's all play. Even when we're doing the work, it's all play. It's all grace. It's all the unfolding of grace. I feel blessed personally. I feel that every moment every opportunity that comes along, and every challenge for that matter, is really a manifestation of that grace. I feel that as I become more and more inwardly peaceful myself, more relaxed, the more I'm able to be that, and the more relaxed and loving I feel with people. My belief is that, at least on an energetic or a vibrational level, inner peace is felt.

Q: What are some of your personal practices for keeping yourself in that consciousness?

For me, it's no longer about a particular practice, though I do advocate meditation. I believe meditation is a very, very good thing and I've been teaching meditation myself since 1976. I believe strongly that it helps center and ground people.

I actually don't feel as if I'm seeking anymore. I feel that a part of me has arrived and the seeking has diminished. I feel very full. I feel very complete. Most of all, I feel very grateful.

Q: *You know, I think that is really the expression of peace at its deepest level. What advice or tip would you give someone who wants to be in that place?*

I love the idea of not betraying your dharma. Most of us feel something that we would really love to do in life, but oftentimes we feel hesitant to pursue. There are a lot of fears and doubts that come up around it. My feeling is that if you are pursuing your dharma in life, or following those natural impulses of consciousness that arise from deep inside, what you do in your daily life can support the growth of that dharma.

Everything you do can support that dharma. I think more and more people—if they follow those natural impulses—find that those are the expressions that life wants them to breathe in the world on a day-to-day basis. The more you follow those impulses, the more you find joy, happiness and all positive qualities bubbling up.

*****

John Raatz is the founder of the Global Alliance for Transformational Entertainment (*www.gatecommunity.org*) and has been involved over the past 21 years in the marketing, PR, distribution and other aspects of groundbreaking films that include *Mindwalk, Baraka, Hearts of Darkness, What the Bleep Do We Know?* and more. His marketing and PR firm, The Visioneering Group, LLC (*www.thevisioneeringgroup.com*), is dedicated to promoting a positive and sustainable future.

*****

Reflection Points

How healthy is your media diet? Notice the music and the messages that surround you in your daily environment.

How could these messages be impacting you consciously and unconsciously?

The Peacebuilder Challenge

Heighten your awareness of toxic or violent messages you are receiving through commercials, music, television or other forms of entertainment. For at least one week, refuse to watch programming that depicts violence as a form of entertainment. Infuse your media diet with healthy, peace-filled alternatives.

16

A POLICY FOR PEACE

Thomas P.M. Barnett

Thomas Barnett is a former assistant for strategic futures in the Office of Force Transformation (OFT) and a professor at the Naval War College. He is the author of The Pentagon's New Map: War and Peace in the 21st Century *and* Great Powers: America and the World After Bush. *Here he discusses political and military strategies for creating peace among nations.*

> "Never bet against a people's desire for freedom, connectivity or pursuit of individual opportunity and liberty, because it is strong."
>
> —Thomas P.M. Barnett, *The Pentagon's New Map*

Q: *Tom, on the very first page of your book* The Pentagon's New Map, *you write: "When the Cold War ended, our real challenge began. The United States had put out so much energy during those years trying to prevent the horror of global war, that it forgot the dream of global peace." Why is it so important for that shift in perspective to occur?*

It is actually crucial now, experiencing, as we are, the first global economic crisis of the globalized age.

You have to go all the way back to 1982 to find a global recession, but back then, we did not really talk about global economy. We really only talked about the West—about 25 percent of humanity at the time, even though it controlled about 70 percent of the global productive power and wealth in the system.

Now we are really talking about a global economy that encompasses, by a lot of measures, upwards of 85 percent of the world's population. Our resource-intensive industrialist model obviously has to change fairly dramatically when you are talking about upwards of 85 to 90 percent of the world's population engaged in pursuing that standard of living.

The reason why it is important for America to shift is that still, very much so, we see a world of nuclear weapons. We see a world of terrorists. We see a world only of bad things. After years of the post-9/11 mindset, America really became disengaged from the way the rest of the world was viewing this time period. It was one of great economic advance, one of incredible integration, networks proliferating, and empowerment to a level that is stunning.

Fifteen to 20 years ago, you could talk about half the world never having used the phone. Now we are talking about Twittering revolutions and cell phone coverage of events almost in any neck of the woods you can name, globally. We really have to understand the way we have conducted ourselves with the world.

Focusing on the prevention of bad things needs to shift into a creation of what has been called "the future worth creating," the recognition that we are coming upon the emergence of a global middle class, which is huge.

This is not an alien world. This is not a Frankenstein that we have unleashed. What we have created here is something we very much sought to do. It went all the way back to the end of the Second World War when Franklin Roosevelt promised a new deal for the rest of the world much as he had created for America, and really made explicit something that had been dreamt of, going all the way back to his cousin Theodore Roosevelt at the turn of the 20th century: this notion of remaking the planet in our image, not so much immediately in a political sense, but very much immediately in the economic sense.

When America had that kind of flowering of integration, what arose in our environment was, for the first time in our history, a broad middle class. We went through a very angry period in our 1870s and 1880s, a populist phase. Even though we were growing very dramatically in terms of wealth, there was great income inequality, raping the environment, child labor abuse, a rough lot for women. It was an angry, divided, unequal society thanks to the progressive movement very much led by religious groups.

Today we are seeing on a global scale many of the same things we went through as a multinational union once we got past our Civil War and the question of slavery in America here from 1865 to 1917.

The role that religious groups played in creating that progressive movement, I believe, is already being replicated on a global scale. That is why we should admit or accept that the 21st century is going to be the most religious century we have ever seen.

Do not put that all in terms of radical fundamentalists. Think more in terms of the evangelicals, who, as a group, are expanding dramatically as fundamentalists are shrinking in their influence. Come to realize that we need to harness that kind of religious awakening much as we did in America at various points. We had a number of religious awakenings in our past. Understand it as a tremendous force for creating a progressive agenda and taming this global version of capitalism that needs to be tamed much as our national versions did 150 years ago.

When people exist in a sustenance mode, just barely getting by, the rules, structures and social codes that come with that mode tend to be really strict: Everybody gets married. Everybody cranks out babies. No homosexuals allowed. We plant these crops. These crops work here. We do not mess around. We do not experiment. This is how we survive the off season.

That is the Malthusian trap that says population is strictly limited because organic growth, how you can grow by using resources from the world, is strictly limited. There is no such thing in that mindset as inorganic growth or escaping the limits of material growth into true wealth like we have done with the Industrial Revolution in the West since the 1800s. Understand that most religions in the world were formed during that tough Malthusian phase. When you allow societies to go from sustenance to abundance, that is a massive social revolution.

Q: And that is what is happening worldwide right now.

That is what is happening worldwide. What happens is what happened in America in the 1870s and the 1880s. We had the rise of the middle class, the rise of leisure activities. That was when all our social and civic institutions really came about, the vast bulk of them. Major league baseball started. All sorts of things happened in that time frame and you are seeing a replication of that model now globally.

These are people who have lived in sustenance for thousands of years, with strict religious codes attached to that survival. All of a sudden, a young woman does not have to marry who dad says. All of a sudden, a young woman does not have to stay in the village. All of a sudden, a young woman can get an education. All of a sudden, she can marry outside her faith, her religion, her race, her social caste, whatever. The controls that had existed and had been enshrined in a lot of tough religious stricture for centuries come under assault and you've got social revolution.

You've got two responses to that social revolution:

One says: Hey, this is out of control. We have not allowed women to do that in our neck of the woods for centuries upon centuries, thousands of years.

One answer is the fundamentalist answer: That it is an evil world. I am going to cut myself off from it. I cannot live with you bad people. I am going to force isolation and drive you out.

Or you say: I need to adapt my religious code to this and my adaptation is going to be the new better version. Then I need to evangelize and spread the word to the rest of the world. If I cannot defeat your integration efforts, I will remake you in my social-religious image.

You see both of these answers coming out of Islam, which is a very rapidly growing religion with a strong evangelical strain to it. But it also has a core fundamentalist-gone-violent strain that really constitutes what most people call this long, persistent struggle against radical extremism. Many people look at that little package and say, "This is our future. Everything is going to hell in a handbasket. More religion is bad."

When you take people from sustenance to abundance, my God, that is a bizarre, perverse journey by their standards. That journey is inescapable because people want better lives. They are going to search for and grab onto self-help guides, religious codes, anything that will give them a moral compass, a hand-hold definition of what a good life is.

You are seeing this in these places like China, which arguably features the most unchurched generation in human history, and a vast one at that. You are seeing China explode in terms of its religiosity, and really go back to what it was, a highly spiritual nation.

Q: I first saw you speak at a spiritual conference and everyone who heard you was abuzz. We are not used to hearing political strategists at conferences of this nature and yet the message really resonated. What is going on with that?

It taps into the bulk of religious sentiment in the world, which tends to be more premillennialist, more optimistic, more like, "How can we make this world more heaven-like over time?"

But do not expect that postmillennialist, fatalistic, rejection-of-the-modern-evil-world mindset to go away immediately. Globalization is definitely still in a very high frontier-integrating mode, much like it was in the American West as we expanded westward across the 19th century.

People are going from sustenance to possibilities of abundance very rapidly. Things are being created out of thin air—networks, governments, opportunities—and there is a huge demand for religion in that kind of landscape, because amidst all that change it supplies a sense of some permanence. It supplies a sense of some code of behavior against which to measure the progress of economics, politics and social change.

If we are in a frontier-integrating mode on a global scale, which I believe we are, it is no surprise that the evangelicals are taking the day, and religions are expanding dramatically. The versions of religion that you find in these frontier areas tend to be more intense than the kind that we have migrated toward in our lasting abundance in the advanced West.

We tend to look at them and say, "Wow, they are scary. They are hardcore. They are old-school. What is up with that?" My Catholic church is certainly getting a taste of that with a lot of these priest shortages. We get these priests from Africa, Latin America, and we expect these laid-back types, but what we get are these firebrands.

Religion, by and large, finds my message unusual in its optimism, and feels empowered with the message that we are in that frontier-integrating age.

I think they like the message that says, "Hey, you are not part of the problem. You are very much part of the solution. Do not let the religious movements of the world be tagged with the radical sins of a very small minority who are on the wane in the historical sense." And yet, as globalization comes to their frontier off-grid locations, you have got to expect them to put up a fight.

Q: *As you were saying, the shift is happening so rapidly that it seems like everybody is trying to catch their footing. It's easy for that Armageddon type of fear to take hold. So here is an alternative to that. It is very refreshing.*

Economic networks tend to race ahead of political networks and/or rules. The economic rules race ahead. The political rules lag behind. The networks race ahead, but the security lags behind. You get kind of a Wild West mentality. We are so removed from our frontier-integrating days; we like things very calm, very certain, very conformed, very controlled.

When we get a package like 9/11, our tendency is to say, "This is either a conspiracy or Armageddon. Either God is in charge or the U.S. government actually pulled this off." The notion that 19 or 20 guys with half a million dollars pulled this off is too scary to contemplate.

So we look for very simple answers, and that is where you get the conspiracy theories. We would prefer to have the stern father administer all the justice in the world, whether it is God or the U.S. government.

You want to fix this world? Then engage this world. Don't put up a firewall.

Q: Thomas, we have talked a lot about peace in a strategic perspective. What does peace mean to you, personally?

It is all about creating certainty. You ask yourself, "What are those various components that people want from their government?" The poor arguably want protection from their circumstances. The rich, you can cynically argue, want protection from the poor.

What the middle class wants is really hard to deliver. That is the challenge of the 21st century when you have a rise of the global middle class. The middle class wants protection from uncertainty. They want protection from the future, which is why they are so drawn to religion.

Religion gives you ideas about the future, a way to contextualize it and say, "If you do this, good things will happen; if you do that, bad things will happen." That's what the middle class wants, because it has achieved a certain standard of living. Its

ambitions are modest. They are middle class, and there is nothing wrong with that.

They want to keep what they have achieved. They want a
better life than their parents had, and they want to pass on the
possibility of better lives to their children. Security has become
the dominant aspect of peace in the last 20 years, and it's a huge
revolution.

When I first got into this business, I had just come from listening to my first child's heartbeat and seeing the ultrasound
when she was a fetus. Then I walked into a room and we had a
discussion about a limited nuclear war.

We had this sassy, rhetorical discussion about how many
tens or hundreds of millions could go in various scenarios and
what would be acceptable.

In the time frame when I started my career 20 years ago, the
paradigm was to light up the planet in seven minutes. Now the
goal is to find, recognize, target and kill one or two bad actors,
try to limit the collateral damage involved, and you try to do
that in about a seven- to eight-minute kill chain, as they call it.
What is stunning about that to me is that in 20 years—this is
human history—we have gone from a paradigm that said
"blow up the planet in seven minutes" to "kill a bad guy in
seven minutes."

So war has shifted from a system-level fear, which was profound when I was a child. We all feared nuclear war. Now it is
down to "get the bad guys." If you look at U.S. military intervention in the last 20 years, all the way back to when we top-
pled Noriega in Panama, we have not fought wars against
militaries much. We have not really waged wars against countries or nations or peoples. Every instance since then, either

right from the start or very soon into it, we realized we were basically there to get the bad guys.

Q: *Can we really get the bad guys or, if we get the bad guys, will there just be another bad guy that pops up?*

This is a good point. The notion that it is not enough to go in and take out the crack dealer, if you leave behind the wife, the six kids and all the associates and all the demand function that guy has created, because two weeks later there will be a new crack dealer.

The same thing you can extrapolate to the level of nations. You take out the bad Saddam, and you can very well end up with another Saddam unless you empower the people.

My argument is, if you do an intervention militarily, you're going to leave that place more connected than you found it. Not just elite-connected through the exporting of resources like energy, but mass-connected. People realize there is an outside world. They realize they should not have to be treated like this. They realize there are other opportunities, and it makes them more demanding of their government, which is a good thing for us.

I grew up in the shadow of the Second World War and everybody I knew who was a man fought in that war. That was a war in which 70 million people were killed. Wars today kill in the hundreds or thousands.

Genocide used to be 7 million or 8 million dead. It is now a couple of hundred thousand dead. It is great that we have ratcheted definitions down, but do not let those ratcheted-down definitions or thresholds convince you that we live in a world of more war today because we do not. We live in the most peaceful planet we have ever had. We have fewer wars. To qualify for a war nowadays, you need three dead a day to get you a thousand dead for a year and they call that a war.

Along those lines you can declare war on everything, can't you? Smoking, choking on toys, whatever. When you get big enough numbers, all sorts of things will give you a war; hence our tendency to declare war on things all the time.

The world lost 28,000 people a day for six years in the Second World War. Now the average war today, in a year, takes about 28,000 lives. So everything has come down from having to defend all the time, and much more to the point of security, watching the economic development, which the middle class wants.

Q: So what about the typical American middle-class person? What can we do to cultivate peace and harmony here in our planet?

You push things like better educational opportunities. Push stricter child labor laws. Push for the improvement of health. You go very green. You tackle global smoking if you want to talk about a global killer. After we drove out all the tobacco companies here in America, they went abroad. They have been enormously successful in hooking a lot of people on smoking.

Anything that promotes the rights of women is crucial because anything that keeps girls in school delays early pregnancy, delays first sex, delays first pregnancy, delays marriage, reduces population pressures, educates them, empowers them, and makes them more uppity and demanding. As we saw in Iran, you really risk your authoritarian regime when you anger the women.

Q: *Well, that makes sense!*

Most authoritarianism usually comes with a very strong patriarchal bent. Yet we know from history, if you want to develop your economy, make your women available to the labor force and deal with all the social changes that come as a result.

Q: *If history has one lesson for us in terms of how to create peace, what is the lesson that you would want to pass on to future generations?*

Connect.

If I would take one perspective from history, I would go with that advice: you should always focus on connection. Never bet against connection. Humans are ultimately highly social animals and whenever they seek connection, so long as it is not harmful to themselves, it should be allowed in each and every instance because with connection typically comes rules.

The freest person on the planet was the Unabomber, living in a shack in the woods, living by his own code, committing murder at will. Why? He had no connection with the outside world.

Every time you take on connection, whether it is a mortgage, a marriage, children, home ownership, career, education, or anything that connects you to the rest of the world, it usually comes with rules; and with those rules comes pacification.

Compared to a history of humanity, what we've got going now is incredibly pacifying. You go back every hundred years in human history, and you will find a much greater percentage of humanity engaged in or preparing for manslaughter.

It is a tremendous thing to realize how much we have ratcheted down violence in the system, and how that has come with all this tremendous wealth. The challenges we face today are fantastically better challenges than we had before.

The answer is still "Connect."

Q: *There is a beautiful quote in your book* Great Powers, *where you write, "I believe life consistently improves for humanity over time, but it does so only because individuals, communities and nations take it upon themselves not only to imagine a future worth creating, but actually try to build it."*

It is the unleashing of the individual ambition on a planetary scale. There has been a massive empowerment and enrichment of hundreds of millions of people around the planet, thanks to globalization's spread. Yes, you will find friction with that process, and if you only focus on the friction with that process, you will ignore the tremendous force that is being unleashed in terms of individual ambition and opportunity.

Yes, there will be violence involved in that. Yes, there will be death and all sorts of tumultuous results. But look at the Balkans 10 years after we bothered to go in and stop the genocide there. The Balkans are a much better place now, connected in all manner—political, economic and social.

Never bet against a people's desire for freedom, connectivity or pursuit of individual opportunity and liberty because it is strong. I admire America for making the effort, even when it does not always do it well. Try to tap into that and unleash it as much as is possible, because when you look at history, there is no other country that has ever tried to do that.

*****

Thomas P.M. Barnett (*www.thomaspmbarnett.com*) is a strategic planner who has worked in national security affairs since the end of the Cold War. A *New York Times* best-selling author and a nationally known public speaker who's been profiled on the front page of the *Wall Street Journal*, Dr. Barnett is in high demand within government circles as a forecaster of global conflict and an expert of globalization, and has been described by *U.S. News & World Report*'s Michael Barone as "one of the most important strategic thinkers of our time." In addition to his speaking and consulting, Tom Barnett is a prolific blogger on current global events where he counts among his tens of thousands of readers representatives from all the major U.S. military commands, virtually all U.S. federal departments, numerous foreign governments, and major research and corporate entities the world over.

*****

Reflection Points

How often do you connect with others outside of your daily sphere of influence?

In what ways could you explore new or deeper connections with people from a diverse economic or cultural background?

The Peacebuilder Challenge

Explore cultural exchange programs that promote global understanding such as Friendship Force (*www.thefriendship-force.org*). Consider hosting a foreign exchange traveler in your home or traveling abroad as a friendship ambassador representing your own country.

17

THE CALL FOR COMPASSION

Mallika Chopra

Mallika Chopra is the founder of Intent.com, a new media company that focuses on personal, social and global development. Her platform leverages technology and social media to connect people in stating and supporting intentions for positive change. The daughter of best-selling author Deepak Chopra, Mallika shares with us the new paradigm for creating a more peaceful world through the World Wide Web.

> "I'm a big believer in action. It's not like you go set an intent and then you don't do anything about it. I think the intent is the first step, and once you have the intent, you start planning out your path to achieving it."
>
> —Mallika Chopra, founder of Intent.com

Q: The United Nations describes three roles we can play to create peace in the world. There are the "peacemakers" who help resolve conflicts. There are the "peacekeepers" who provide stability and infrastructure for peace following conflict resolution. The role we are focusing on with Let It Begin With Me *is the role of the "peacebuilder." Peacebuilders create environments where peace can thrive, where abundance can thrive, where joy can thrive. What I'm seeing with your company, Intent.com, is that it really provides a great place for people to go and heal. It's an online resource for helping people feel support and love.*

Absolutely. I think when people feel that love and support, then they want to give it as well. Our site is a very active community, and we're seeing people love to support each other. It is great.

Q: *What is the impact that this site can have globally just by helping people connect with people?*

That's something that we are really excited about accomplishing. I have a really small team that works on the site and we've really tried to make it very organic and grassroots. We let it grow at its own pace because our goal is really to create a long-term, sustainable resource for people.

It's not a quick fix. The future holds so much uncertainty. I've grown up always believing that. But we're already seeing some great stories coming out of this.

Q: *Mallika, what was your inspiration behind launching Intent.com?*

I think having an intent is the first step in anyone's path to wellness. We like to define wellness in personal terms of healthy living, healthy relationships, and finding success in your life. But also we see wellness in terms of society—human rights and social rights. And there is also wellness in terms of Mother Earth and our planet and the spirit. Intent.com really is that first step.

The inspiration behind the website was really my personal background, growing up as the daughter of Deepak Chopra, and interacting with so many interesting people and voices from around the world. I met many people who are doing such incredible work in trying to bring together a global community of people who have good intentions and who can help pave the way.

Q: When you go to Intent.com, it asks what your intention is. You can type in your own intention for the day and see what other people have intended as well. What is your intention today?

I continue to put in new intents daily. Today my intent is to let go of past grievances and focus on building bridges for the future. This is really based on whatever I'm going through. Whether I do this once a day or several times a day, I find that entering my intent into the web page, and thus into the ethers and the universe, provides an anchor for me for the rest of the day.

I'd like to give an example. I was going through a lot of stress. We're a startup company and we had a stressful situation. I put in my intent that I'm going to remain calm in the midst of the storm. Just putting that out there and getting so many people who supported my intent or gave me recommendations really helped me get through the chaotic period of those few days.

We're finding that people get a lot of inspiration and comfort from stating their intent and getting support from other people. The whole system allows people to support your intents, comment on them and share them.

Q: Yes, it is very powerful. I went in there today and posted my intent. It's a wonderful, clarifying tool just to think, Okay, what really is my intention for today? Do you have people who are using it that way as a daily tool or spiritual practice?

It's amazing. Intent has always played a really important role. When we first started, it was really a hobby where I had all these friends blogging on the site and it just grew. We started off aggregating all of the best voices around the planet on personal, social and global wellness. I'm very fortunate because obviously my father participated, and also many of his friends who are well-known.

That was what I thought I could be of service doing. Of course, the content is amazing. What we are finding on the site, which is most exciting, is that the individual intents have become the most viral aspects. People are posting their intent several times a day. We've also integrated it with things like Twitter and Facebook, so by adding your intent, you can spread it to more people. We have this simple button there that says "Support" and people just love to support each other.

Q: Yes, I think you're absolutely right. The focusing aspect is one piece of it, but the community support is incredibly powerful. It's wonderful to be able to not only receive that, but to be able to give it as well.

We have one page which is just intentions. It's inspiring.

It really is a very positive and empowering kind of community that's developing. That, to me, has been the best development. It has gone from being a blog, where we have really interesting people writing, to a website combined with intent. And now whenever you put in your intent, you'll also easily find the content related to that intent from many great bloggers. We'll be integrating that more and more.

Q: *Are the users able to submit content as well?*

Yes, and that's what is wonderful because we get so much from them. It's such fantastic content. I started off getting all these *New York Times* best-selling authors, people like Archbishop Desmond Tutu and these kinds of role models from all over the world who are all so inspiring and great. But now what we're finding is that some of the best content and, in fact, often the most popular content, is actually coming from members of the Intent.com community.

So anybody can come to Intent. Anybody can put in their intent and anyone can blog on Intent. We program the homepage daily, but really the rest of the website is very much whatever the latest posts are. It really is democratic, I would say. We find that people in the community find something and then they spread it themselves. They use Facebook and Twitter and email their friends if they find something that inspires them.

Again, my dad may be embarrassed to know this, but by far, he is not the most popular person on the site. Some of the most popular content is actually user content, which for us is very thrilling.

Q: *It seems to indicate a major shift that's going on in the world right now regarding where the expertise is really coming from. It seems inner knowledge is just pouring forth from the person next door, the person who sits next to you at church. What are some of the changes that you're noticing as you put this together?*

We have great experts on the site and I don't want to undervalue that. But I'd like to give the example of how our readers are bringing value to each other: I'm a mom with two young kids, and one of the big challenges in my life is always finding balance with just being a good mom and a working mom.

I'd say that any mom can be stretched in a million directions. So I'm always trying to figure out how to deal with that. I put my intention out there to be a good mom and then another mom, who is not a parenting expert, wrote, "Have you tried turning your cell phone off from 6 to 9 p.m. so that when you're with your children, you're actually present with your children rather than being distracted by the computer or your cell phone?"

All the practical advice I get is the most impactful, and it comes because I shared my intent.

Those are the kinds of things that personally get me really excited. The site is doing well. We're getting a lot of traffic. We're getting a lot of pickup, but I think what's the most fulfilling is to see that the community is driving it.

Q: There are many spiritual practices. You decided to focus on the power of intention. Why do you think intention is such a powerful tool?

I was very young when my father started meditating and started his spiritual journey. This was when I was 9 and my brother was 5, and we were very fortunate to get meditation as a tool early on in our life. I think meditation helped us find silence and a connection to Spirit. One of the things my parents used to do with my brother and me when we were still young was to have us set intentions about what we wanted in our life and how we wanted to serve in our life. From a very young age, that power of intention was honed into us.

When I became pregnant, I found that it was a very important time for me to set my personal intentions as a mom. My personal journey in self-development really started when I was becoming a mother. Even though I'd grown up in this environment of spirituality and I meditated and had all these tools, I really wasn't into it. It was "my dad's thing."

Then, when I became pregnant, suddenly I became engaged in thinking about who I am and where I have come from. This notion of intention really played into my life at that time. I actually wrote a book called *100 Promises to My Baby*, and those are basically 100 intentions about how I want to serve as a mom.

When I decided to launch the site, I really wanted Intent.com to be the brand because I felt it really represented that first step toward well-being.

Q: I love the idea of 100 Promises to My Baby. *It seems that wherever we are in life, it could be 100 Promises to My Partner or 100 Promises to Myself. To be able to reference intentions like that is extremely powerful. What do you think is the power in setting the intention, and then how often do you go back to that intention?*

I think intents are very different from goals. I see intents as planting the seeds of who we aspire to be, just like you would plant a seed of a flower or plant. You don't dig it up every day. You plant that seed, and then you water it, nurture it and take care of it. And then it grows.

I think setting the intent is the first step to getting somewhere. Then after you set your intent, you start setting goals about how to achieve it. Intent is that deeper first step. By setting the intention, we actually start the process of realizing it as well.

I was taught my entire life about setting clear intentions, which is also why we've kept them short. When you go and you put your intent on our site, it's best to keep them as one-sentence affirmations so that you can really crystallize your thought or a desire and action in that one sentence. That's where we start on our site: what the intent is. Being concise helps us encapsulate the essence of our hopes and desires.

I'm a big believer in actions as well. It's not like you go set an intent and then you don't do anything about it. But I think the intent is that first step. Once you have the intent, you can start planning out your path to achieving it.

Q: It seems that right now is the perfect time for a concept like yours. The technology is there. The consciousness is there. It seems everything is coming together for this particular time in our history.

Yes. It's amazing. Ten years ago, we had to spend so much money on technology. It was a very different time. Today what's amazing is that it's really just putting together tools that are already out there.

It's absolutely global. Wherever people are in the world, they hear similar intent for their own healthy lives, for good relationships, for a compassionate society, and to live on a planet that's healthy. We may approach it in different ways, but I think fundamentally, people are seeking wellness in their lives and that it is really a global phenomenon. What the Internet allows us to do is really connect globally.

Q: Your intention behind the site is wellness in every aspect of the word. It's wellness within. It's wellness for the planet. What is your intention for some of these different aspects?

I have grown up seeing all these. I was very fortunate to be exposed to really inspiring people, including best-selling authors, teachers, politicians and celebrities. But most important, I saw so many other people through my father's world who are basically on a journey of self-discovery. They often entered their journey from some pain, such as going through a divorce, being diagnosed with a disease, or losing a loved one.

I grew up seeing people in their healing process and seeing so many incredible people from around the world who could help. I think that the original intent of the site was to bring together all these incredible voices.

What we're seeing on the site now is that we are not only bringing these great voices together, but what's even more effective is the community that is corralling around people. Just this weekend we had a scary situation on our site where I think someone was in extreme pain and actually put some messages on the site that were very concerning about his own life.

I was contacted through the community—people from South America and other places who were able to tell us that this person was in pain, more extreme than we would normally face. But it was really the community that was writing to him, supporting him and helping us find a way to reach out to people in his community. That's what is inspiring to me. It's the community that is coming forth to support each other.

Q: That must be incredibly fulfilling to you to see your vision come about. There couldn't be a more profound impact that you could have in a person's life.

Yes, exactly. At the end of the day, my father says that what fulfills him has been the ability to help people heal. If Intent.com can now play its role through technology to help people, that is so fulfilling to me.

Q: Mallika, we have been talking about the new generation emerging, not just in terms of age, but about the shift that is happening on the planet. Business is being done differently. Connection, spirituality, everything is being done in a new way. What do you think the role of this next generation is in the wellness and spirituality aspects of the world?

When I started my first company 10 years ago, it was a very different time. I think that society and business were in a different place. Frankly it was a harder path to forge. In the last five to seven years, we've seen the Green Movement. People are becoming more aware. Business has also gotten on board. Everybody now has their own sustainability initiative. It's now the cool thing to do.

I think people have become more empowered on a mass level. They're taking control and taking responsibility for their communities and what's happening.

We've seen many things merge with Intent.com. We really began redefining wellness as something that's personal, social, global and spiritual. We cannot separate our personal wellness from the wellness of society and Mother Earth. I think we're seeing that in business.

The other thing that's really interesting since I started this company is that I have mainstream media with big media companies and mainstream advertisers. They're all saying, "Look, we know that wellness is important, but we don't necessarily know how to integrate that."

For example, our first advertising campaign on Intent.com was SunChips. They're a big media company, but they're really saying, "Okay, we're creating this compostable bag. How can we be more socially responsible?" I know that there are other companies, traditional Madison Avenue companies, that are really trying to shift in a real way; for example, shift the ingredients in their recipes, become more socially responsible, or incorporate more sustainable practices.

I think it is happening. It will take time, but it is starting to really happen.

Q: The entire change process seems to be accelerating. In fact, I think those people who are not in on it now have people looking to them and asking, "Why not?"

Yes. What we've seen in the past was greed. We've seen that coming from company leadership. That's just not acceptable anymore. People don't have patience for it.

There has been an upsurge of what we're calling spiritually motivated social action. I think we've reached a level of consciousness as a movement where the next obvious step is taking it out into the world and making as big a difference as we possibly can.

Q: That's an important part of your site — social and global. What do you have there that can really support people in their spiritual journey?

Again, it comes from who we are personally. I've seen that with my father. My father started off talking about health, very much coming from a doctor's perspective. But in the last few years, he's really evolved to really looking at conflict resolution, human rights and some of the really significant social situations. It's something that's been an issue for me for many years. Human rights, social rights and issues like hunger, malaria, child abuse and taking care of Mother Earth—these are all part of our personal well-being. We cannot be separate from what's happening in society.

Q: I think a lot of us have been searching for the balance between spirituality and social activism. Our spiritual nature tells us, "Hold it in prayer." Yes, that's an incredibly powerful step — one place to begin. It seems that when we are prayed up, our actions come from a very different place.

Yes, I think you are right. If we incorporate spirituality into our life and that influences right decisions, then we are led to the right action and the right words. But one of the things that I've seen growing up in this movement is that people often then just escape. They use spirituality as an escape mechanism to justify that it's not really pain or it's not really suffering. Again, for those who are going through it, we really have to be compassionate and really reach out very actively beyond ourselves.

Q: Whether it's through Intent.com or other gatherings, there seems to be a coming together of like-minded people who are now saying, "I know this shift is happening. I know that I'm a part of it. How do I serve?" Are you feeling that?

Yes, we definitely are feeling it, and we're finding that it is a global movement. We're connecting and engaging people literally from Argentina to South Africa, from Mongolia to Australia. This actually creates a lot of hope for our future.

*****

Mallika Chopra (*www.intent.com*) has spent the last 10 years working in a variety of capacities in the media world. Her strengths in creating creative content combined with strategic and marketing thinking has allowed her to successfully fuel an entrepreneurial drive in a number of arenas. As part of her work with her book *100 Promises to My Baby*, she serves as a spokesperson for UNICEF, raising awareness for orphans who have been affected by HIV and AIDS.

*****

Reflection Points

What is your intent for today?

How could you indicate your support for the people in your life as they seek to turn their intentions into reality?

The Peacebuilder Challenge

Share your intent with others by posting it free at *www.intent.com.*

18

THE ANSWER IS THE QUESTION

Wendy Craig-Purcell

Rev. Wendy Craig-Purcell is a spiritual leader, world peace activist, and author of Ask Yourself This! Questions to Open the Heart, Expand the Mind and Awaken the Soul. *Wendy teaches that the path to both inner and outer peace begins by asking deep, probing questions of ourselves. In the conversation that follows, she shares these questions, and how we can use them in every area of our life to resolve conflict and establish harmony.*

> "Peace to me is a state of harmony within myself where there is no warring faction, where there is centeredness and joyfulness in my thinking. There is congruency in what I believe, how I live, how I talk and the choices that I make."
>
> —Wendy Craig-Purcell, author of *Ask Yourself This!*

Q: Your book Ask Yourself This! *provides some thought-provoking questions. Tell us why the questions are just as important as, maybe even more important than, the answers, when we come together to build a world of peace.*

I think the reason that questions are so important, Mindy, is that they are actually channels through which our mental, emotional and creative energy flows. The quality of the answers we receive is directly related to the quality and the timing of the questions that we ask ourselves.

So the deeper answers that we get when we ask really good questions open a path to create our lives consciously by design, rather than by default. The questions we ask are critically important.

Q: *It seems the questions really help us to step out of the old patterns and into a new level of awareness. How do you use questions in your own life?*

I've used them to help me probe deeper into the very heart and core of what's really important to me. For many of us, we were taught in school the importance of getting the right answer for the test. While the right answers in life certainly are important, we can't get the right answer if we're not asking the right question.

So often, when we find ourselves in difficult or challenging situations in our life, we get caught on the problematic level of things. If we can step aside, look from a wider perspective and from a spiritual point of view, and begin to ask ourselves a different set of questions, we find that we're able to tap into the innate wisdom that's within us. But it's only there if we ask the right question at the right time.

Q: *I think the questions are so powerful, not just for the individual for our spiritual practice, but it seems also a really great way to connect with our community, to connect with our families. What are* *some ways people can use these questions in their outer world, in the workplace, and in their family lives?*

I think in the workplace, it might be fun, say, over a lunch hour to pick a couple of questions that are just particularly meaningful to the individual or to the organization and begin to share first responses to those questions—but then not to just settle with the first response. I think that it's important that we allow some of the provocative questions that I pose in the book to settle more deeply.

For example, the question, "What am I saying *Yes!* to in my life?" Our lives are the outpicturing of our thoughts, our feelings and our choices. As we look out into our world, we see and manifest form. What is it that we have been consciously or unconsciously welcoming into our life, saying *Yes!* to, whether it's individually, in the workplace, or at home?

It helps us to see our lives in new and different ways. And when we see our lives in new and different ways, we can change direction. We can change course.

Q: As I think about my family, my relationships and my marriage, these questions can be powerful tools to create more harmony in the home and to create more harmony in our relationships. In a nonconfrontational way, it can really open up some meaningful dialogues. Have you experienced that?

Absolutely. In a family dynamic, when you're facing different choices as a family, you can ask, "Is it faith or fear that's guiding us? Are we moving in the direction of what is new, possible, hopeful and life-giving, or are we stuck in the past, limited in our thinking and responding from a place of fear?"

What a dialogue to have, not only with your spouse or significant other, but to invite children into that kind of inquiry!

Just posing the question "Is it faith or fear guiding me?" is powerful. It automatically points to what we're giving our attention to.

Q: *Imagine sitting around the dinner table with the family and going through some of these questions. The dialogue really gets families, individuals and communities connected in a much deeper way. That is one of the important steps to creating a more peaceful world. When you think about peace, what does peace mean to you?*

To me, peace is a state of harmony within myself where there is no warring faction, where there is centeredness and joyfulness in my thinking. There is congruency in what I believe, how I live, how I talk and the choices that I make. On the individual level, it is an outpicturing of compassion and kindness.

In terms of family dynamics, it would involve how it is that we relate to one another, what it is that we hold as possible for one another. On very basic levels, it is to cause no harm in any way, whether it is with our words, our thoughts or our actions. In fact, Mindy, one of the questions in the book that kind of speaks to this is the question "How safe is it for people to walk in the corridors of my mind?"

Q: *Oh, that's a great question.*

Isn't it? For many of us in spiritual practice, we have certainly committed ourselves to living a nonviolent life. We don't use physical force, manipulation or those kinds of tactics to get our way. Yet there is an even deeper level of peacefulness that has to do with the quality of the thinking that we hold toward one another, how judgmental and how critical we are in private.

If we truly do believe that our thoughts are things and that what we hold silently within us emanates outwardly, then that's the next level of our practice. It's not just to stop being physically violent in the world. It's to stop the emotional and mental violence within us.

Q: You bring up a great point. As we think about creating peace in the world, what are some of the most important questions we should be asking ourselves?

I think the question "If I could solve the *how*, what would I do?" is an important question, both personally and in our society.

We all want a peaceful world. We want a world that works for everyone, with no one and nothing left out. Why we get stuck sometimes is because we haven't quite figured out how to do all of that. We diminish our energy and our focus on working toward the vision. We get so stuck in the *how*.

First we have to get really, really clear about what is it that we most want. We then commit ourselves to knowing that we free up energy when we make an absolute commitment that we are creating a peaceful world that works for everyone. We free up energy to figure out: How are we going to do that? How do we need to vote to support that? What are our lifestyle choices that we have to make that support a more peaceful, equitable world? What are the games that we allow our children to play? What are the products that we buy or that we don't buy?

Q: Talk about the use of questions in your spiritual practice. How do you use them? How can people take this on as something that helps them enrich their spiritual life?

The very act of asking deep, probing questions changes our life spiritually. I broke the book apart into seven chapters and a bonus chapter. I looked at key areas of life and living. I looked at questions that can help one grow personally. In one section, the book has questions that can help one grow spiritually in self-knowledge.

Perhaps sitting down first, being quiet with the book, considering what area of your life you most want to either explore or to improve, and then find the chapter that corresponds most closely to that. It may be the chapter that deals with spirituality or it might be another. I would read the chapter, and then I would look at the questions within that chapter that seem to really grab my heart and soul.

Then I would do a couple of things with them: I would commit them to memory. I would use them in my quiet time by silently asking myself that particular question, listening and noticing what comes up, and not just accepting the first answer or the first response, because a lot of times our top-of-mind thinking is just that. It's not the deeper core of what's really moving within us.

I would still take note of what that first response is. But then, I would ask the question again at a deeper level, and ask, *What next?* and *What next?* with each question. Then I would journal. I would look back over a period of a couple of weeks and begin to see what patterns were emerging.

Q: *That's really powerful. What are some ways we can use this as we are consciously creating a world of peace?*

One of my favorite questions is "What is this telling me about me?"

I find myself asking that question when I notice that I'm feeling irritated. I might feel annoyed by something that someone has said, done or not done. I know that when I'm upset, I'm not at peace. I need to avoid the very human temptation to make it about the other person and to blame the other person. I've trained myself so much in this.

Almost my first response when I notice that upset is to ask myself, "Alright, Wendy, what is this telling me about me right now? What's getting triggered? Why am I having the response that I'm having?" What I've learned over time, Mindy, is that the willingness to ask that question of myself automatically begins to bring me to a more centered state and usually very quickly. I'll identify what has been triggered. Am I feeling afraid? Am I feeling rushed? Am I feeling left out, disappointed or whatever the particular thing may be?

But the willingness, once I notice the upset, to ask that deeper question "What is this telling me about me?" helps me make a conscious choice to move into a state of peacefulness that I wouldn't have moved into had I just noticed the upset and not probed a little deeper.

*****

Wendy Craig-Purcell (*www.wendycraigpurcell.com*) is the founding minister of the Unity Center in San Diego, California, and an active participant in the Association for Global New Thought (AGNT). Craig-Purcell participated in three "Synthesis Dialogues," which brought together a number of the world's principal thought leaders to dialogue with His Holiness the Dalai Lama of Tibet. She has participated in the production of six large-scale "Awakened World" conferences and the Gandhi King Peace Train and Living Legends of Nonviolence Conference. Craig-Purcell and her family have traveled the world, and contributed to the building of two schools in the Republic of Malawi in southeast Africa. Wendy continues to donate time and resources to help the needs of others across the globe.

*****

Reflection Points

Reflect upon the questions Wendy discussed: How safe is it for people to walk in the corridors of my mind?

If I could solve the *how*, what would I do?

The Peacebuilder Challenge

Keep a journal where you can respond to these kinds of probing questions. Write your first responses. Then, as you further reflect, capture the additional ideas and insights that come to mind. Review your writings each week to notice patterns that emerge.

19

CREATING PEACE ENVIRONMENTS

Jim Bunch

Whether it is launching a new business venture or helping someone upgrade their life, there is a common thread you will find with Jim Bunch: bringing out the best in the companies and people that he works with, while personally maintaining an ultimate life. The creator of the business and personal development program called The Ultimate Game of Life, Jim speaks with us about how we can create environments for peace.

> "I think people are returning to what is really important. I am starting to notice that people are looking in each other's eyes again. They are starting to want to connect."
>
> —Jim Bunch, The Ultimate Game of Life

Q: Jim, you have created a program called The Ultimate Game of Life, TUG for short. Share with us what your perspective is on life as a game.

For many years, I was very serious about this thing called Life. Then I actually saw a comedian one time who put things into perspective. He said, "You know, people, you need to quit taking life so seriously. It is not like you are going to get out alive anyways." So it just kind of hit me.

What we say often is "How you do games is often how you do life." So you will see how people respond to money, or how they respond to relationships, or how they respond just to happiness or peace. If you put them in an environment where there are games that are designed, they will do the same thing in the game that they do in life.

Q: I have heard it said, "How we do anything is how we do everything." So it is a great metaphor. TUG offers a great chance to really take on whatever we are trying to create in life from the perspective of it being a game, and that keeps it light and fun. How do we use this to pursue a goal like peace?

When you look at global peace, you have to pare it down and simplify it. If we are expecting to create a planet full of peaceful beings, we have to look at the inner game of peace, the outer game of peace, and then the global game as well.

That inner game is when we talk about your inner architecture, your self. In other words, it is the relationship you have with your thoughts, your beliefs, your values, your gifts, your talents, and how you have designed your inner game. That, for many people, is a source of contention and conflict until they understand that, first off, they have this thing called *beliefs*.

Beliefs are the filters through which we see the rest of the world. If I believe that life is good, then I am going to see everything in life as good. If I believe that life is a struggle, then I am going to see the world and all the people in it as a struggle. If you are not aware that that is just a belief system, then that is your reality.

Phase one is to recognize that part of the inner game is understanding we have this thing called beliefs. In the Game, we call it the *memetics*.

Memetics stands for "means," which are these beliefs that are handed down from generation to generation to generation.

Q: How do you know the right memetics to hold?

Well, I think you have to look at the results. Do your beliefs give you the results you want? I look at it in three areas of your life: Are you happy, are you healthy, and are you wealthy?

So once you start looking at people's results in terms of happiness, health and wealth, it simplifies the game. Then you simply ask them if they have designed a game that they can win. Have they set themselves up to be somebody who is what we call an "ultimate player"? Are they winning the inner and outer game of life?

Q: You talked about inner, outer and global peace. So if we begin with people who are happy, healthy and wealthy, do we create societies, communities, nations, a world of happiness, health and abundance?

That would be the ideal. I personally have not been able to see another way that we can get to global peace unless we have people who are actually peaceful and happy with their own life. When I look at the cause of war, the cause of murder, the cause of crime, or any of these things, it is because inside there is some kind of anger, rage or disconnect that is causing people to feel that the best solution is to harm another.

Look at cultures right now that are teaching their children to strap bombs on themselves. What is the only way that you can do that? You raise them in an environment where you control their beliefs. You design their belief system to believe that this is the best thing they could do with their precious life. The child knows no difference.

A hundred years ago, the impact of having limiting beliefs was not as great as it is today. The speed at which thought moves today around the planet is so much faster. Three and a half billion people around the planet are now connected through mobile devices. What does this mean as far as global peace?

We now have access to anyone and everyone around the planet. Our thoughts, our beliefs and our actions are being impressed around the whole planet instantaneously. Look at Twitter. Look at Facebook. Facebook has more than 250 million people right now. The Internet is providing a global communication platform that is not driven by a few, but is driven by many. Along with that, we have a situation for the first time in our history where we have some problems that are big enough that we as a planet have to play together.

Q: I think a lot of us have been doing the inner work for a while and we have become aware that we are stuck. We find ourselves doing the same thing. I find myself doing the same thing over and over again. So how do you change?

I call this the three A's. The first is to raise your *awareness*. The second is *action*, and the third is *accountability*. Now, again, everybody would say, "Of course, I need to take new actions. I need to be held accountable to a new higher standard."

But most people are missing the simple distinction that trying to change your behavior using willpower often will not work. It makes sense if you understand the concept called the

Nine Environments of You. The environments are stronger than your willpower.

The simple reason is that these nine environments are on 24 hours a day, seven days a week, but your willpower, which is a mental faculty, is only on when you are focused on it.

The challenge is when people set goals or they want to change a habit or a behavior, they want to start being nice to somebody that they were not nice to before, they want to start exercising when they have not been doing it for three, four, five, six, seven, 10 years ... they are trying to use willpower to get them to change. But the environments they have designed, both internally and externally, are creating habits and patterns that are holding them steady or stuck.

If we can teach the Nine Environments, not only will we be able to create that inner peace for ourselves—because now we can start to line up our inner world to reflect or match our outer world—but we can also work from the outer world inside because it is not just a one-way street.

We need to make sure that we are working on the inner game and the outer game simultaneously. Otherwise, what happens is I listen to my affirmations, I look at my vision board, I listen to great preachers or speakers or people like that, and the information comes in, but it does not match up with the rest of my reality. So it becomes what I call the personal development drug of "hopium." You know a lot of people who are super excited but completely disempowered within a few days after hearing an inspiring message.

We encourage a different approach to life. Let's say you and I are going to become yoga masters or experts. We can either go to a yoga class for the next 10 years and try to learn all 12 poses in each of our 60-minute sessions two or three times a week. Or we can simply say, "You know what? I am going to try the first pose for the next 30 days for five minutes a day." What you will find is by simplifying your game, you will actually become a master instead of a dabbler. Simplicity succeeds and complexity kills.

What is great about that too is that we think, Five minutes day ... I can do that! It is a win versus setting a huge objective or goal and then feeling like you failed.

Q: Yes. That is what most people do, especially overachievers, right?

We are taught: Go for the biggest dream, the biggest vision, the biggest goal. I agree. You want to have the big vision, the big goal, the big mission. But putting yourself into a state or vibration of winning every day will cut your expectations in half, and then you overachieve.

So let us talk about the Nine Environments. First off, the benefits of understanding these nine environments is that you will start to achieve your goals more effortlessly, efficiently and effectively. You will no longer have to rely on willpower to get the job done and—here is the real kicker—you will no longer rely completely on yourself to reach your goals. If you design your environments properly, they become your partners in goal achievement.

Q: Talk about what you mean by "environments." When I hear the word "environment," I typically think of my physical surroundings.

Sure. The first part we talk about is called Y-O-U. Now Y-O-U is you. That is the part of you that is unchanging. It is the universal energy or spirit or life force or connection that runs through every physical or human body that animates or brings life to this body. That is not one of the Nine Environments. It is the part of you that is unchanging.

Q: That is the center of it all.

Exactly. Surrounding Y-O-U there are your memetics, or core beliefs. These are the filters through which you see the world.

We have beliefs about all nine environments. We will start with the easiest one which is called the *Physical Environment*. A lot of people do not realize the impact that their physical environment has on the way that they think, the way that they feel and the way that they act. Have you ever walked into an office and there is clutter and chaos, or there is stuff everywhere?

What does that do to you and the way you think and feel? It instantly scatters your mind, right? So you can be walking in, crystal clear and focused, and all of a sudden there is chaos in the room. That instantly affects the way you think and feel.

Here is the crazy thing: Your physical environment is always surrounding you. No matter where you go. Most people bounce between three primary environments: their home, since they sleep, eat and live there; their office; and their vehicle.

If you think about it, there are places, environments, where you walk in and you instantly feel at peace. There is beauty, there is sacredness. You could just feel that there is something different there. Friendliness.

Q: The physical environment is really one of my favorites because it is just so easy to clean my office, light a candle, turn on some music, burn some incense and—boom!—I am at peace. Talk about some of the others because some of the others are a little more challenging.

Let us talk about the *Financial Environment*. Financial is not just money. It could be the team that you have or have not built. It could be software that you use. It could be currencies.

If you structured your beliefs properly, then you are at peace with finances. If not, you may be experiencing worry or doubt or frustration or fear or scarcity or any of these things. What that tells us is you have designed a belief system that promotes a financial environment called doubt, fear or scarcity.

The next one is called your *Network Environment*. Often we say that your net worth is related to your network. In other words, if you look at the people that you surround yourself with, ask yourself: Have they created the kind of life that I want? Are they truly happy, healthy and wealthy?

Your network is an association you belong to like a church or maybe the PTA, a sports or athletic association, or even a social network like a Facebook or Twitter. If you were to map out all the people in your network and then look at how they live, odds are your life is somewhat a reflection of those people. Are they into personal growth and development? Are they into spirituality? Are they into causing frustration and pain and suffering in people's lives?

The next one is called your *Relationships Environment*. Relationships are your family, friends, close colleagues, your personal support system. This is a closer, more intimate network. We all know that if things are going wrong in your relationships, whether it is with a spouse or a loved one, or maybe someone is sick or someone is just mentally or emotionally disturbed, that has an impact on our Game of Life. This can be one of the tougher ones for people to deal with.

The next one is your *Body Environment*. When we talk about the body, we are talking about not only your physical body, but we are talking about health and energy and things like this. If your health goes, it does not matter what you are doing because the game on the physical plane is now done. If you have the right energy to create world peace, you take care of your health and become an example of health. As one of my friends says, "You should treat your body like a temple, not like a play-ground."

We had some amazing results with people starting in that area too. We have one woman, for example, who was quite a bit overweight and not in the habit of exercising. I told her not to try to do too much at once. Simplify. So she started walking on a treadmill at one mile per hour for one minute a day. A year later, she had lost over 80 pounds. She got on a call with us and she said, "Jim, I am so excited. I just got off the treadmill at two miles an hour (double the speed) for 60 minutes and I feel I could keep going."

These are the kind of things that will happen if you just start off simple. You will create new habits and create long-term, sustainable change. This is important. We are looking at global peace not for an instant but for eternity. It does no good for us to have one day of peace then go back to 364 days of chaos.

This next one is one of my favorite environments. We call it the *Self Environment*. This one is what we call an intangible. You cannot see, hear, smell, taste or touch it. It is like the wind. You cannot see the wind but you can see the effects of the wind when it blows across a tree. Well, your self environment is that internal part of you. It is your personality. It is your gifts, your talents, your strength. It is your emotion.

It is also what I call your internal architecture. So this is where you hold your vision, your values, your life purpose, and your legacy. Those all fall into the self environment. Your self-image is your belief about your self environment.

When one person looks in the mirror, they see somebody who is loving and compassionate and inspiring and engaging. That same person, on a bad day, can look in the mirror and think, You are a loser. You are not worth anything. That is your self environment. Keep in mind that all of these environments we see through our memetics or beliefs.

Q: Yes. I've heard it said, "Do not believe everything you think." I have a lot of thoughts that would not make for good beliefs.

My first step goal with people is for them to be aware that they have beliefs. The second step is to get them to upgrade those beliefs, turning a limiting belief into an empowering belief. Then eventually, if they are really into mastering the Game of Life, my hope is to get them to the place where they no longer believe in beliefs at all. Your belief system is simply a made-up paradigm. It can pull you up, but eventually the very thing that pulled you up becomes your ceiling.

That leads us to the next environment called the *Spiritual Environment*. Again, memetics play an interesting role. More blood has been spilled on this planet because of religion, the belief systems around spirituality, than anything else.

The challenge here is that when belief systems clash and people believe that they are right and someone else is wrong, they will do crazy things. If you strip all the beliefs away and you look at the core messages of most of the major religions or spiritual practices around the world, many of them would have similar messages.

They want to connect you to a higher power. They want you to do right by other humans in some way, shape or form.

Ultimately, we would love to see people connected. One of the biggest core needs of humans is to feel connected with each other. The reason that I love sharing this concept of the Nine Environments with people is that it gives them a road map to not only analyze their current life, but to finally start to connect to other people and improve all of our lives.

Q: Jim, bring it all together for us. How do these Nine Environments work together to create inner peace, outer peace, global peace?

When you are designing your ultimate life, it is not just about de-cluttering or reading a new book or listening to a tape. The idea here is that we want you to start to play a very big game. We want you to look closely at how your environments can pull you like a vacuum into this bigger direction or this bigger game.

If I design my environments properly, they should pull me to my future instead of me having to push and struggle and force my way to a bigger future.

The other thing to understand is that you can design environments, you can change existing environments, you can influence them, or you can remove yourselves from them altogether. If you have environments that are destructive or not working, you may just have to eliminate those environments altogether.

Now I do not mean take somebody out, which I have had many husbands and wives jokingly ask about. I mean simply remove yourself from the environment until you are strong enough and stable enough to go back into that environment and be the change that you wish to see in that environment.

So when you are designing your life, whether it is your personal life or your business life, ask yourself: How do I upgrade each of these different areas so that I have the best team on board in my finances, so that I have couples around me in relationships that are empowering and inspiring me, instead of constantly talking about what is not going right? How do I put myself in an athletic circle of people who are taking incredible care of their physical body because they respect their body instead of trashing their body?

Q: Jim, we have talked about the individual journey and all that we can do and how it manifests in the outer world, but what is your perspective on the reality of achieving peace in our lifetime?

If everybody on the planet understood each others' core values, we would start to see how global peace is possible. We would finally feel good about life and the way that we are living it. If they do not have that, all of the goal setting and things like that are irrelevant.

People are returning to what is really important. People are looking at each other's eyes again. They are starting to want to connect with people. They are starting to care again. They are not as wrapped up in the stuff that we have, but more engaged in who we are.

This discovery of who we are is, I think, one of the first steps to us creating global peace. If we could help every single person on the planet understand their values, their strengths, their gifts, their talents and what they can contribute to the world, they would feel valued. We can finally play a game in which we can all win.

*****

Jim Bunch (*www.jimbunch.com*) is on a mission to inspire happiness, health and wealth worldwide. The creator of the life coaching program The Ultimate Game of Life (*www.theultimategameoflife.com*), Jim shares his knowledge, experience and passion to help people create their ultimate lives and businesses. He shares a vision for a world where people and the planet understand and act upon the truth that we are truly all connected—and our existence is dependent on this reality. Through his work, he is helping men, women and children know their strengths, gifts and talents and how they can then share those openly with their local and global communities.

*****

Reflection Points

Which of the environments that Jim discussed are best supporting you in living a life of peace and abundance?

Which ones provide for you the most opportunity for growth?

The Peacebuilder Challenge

Download Jim's free nine-part video introduction to the Nine Environments at *www.theultimategameoflife.com.* Choose one of the Nine Environments to focus on for the next 30 days. Take one small action a day related to improving that environment.

20

PEACELICIOUS!

Donna Collins

Donna Collins is the executive director of the Global Peace Project and a woman who is known for bringing people together with delicious meals that are good for the body, the planet and the soul. She shares with us how every meal and every morsel is an opportunity to celebrate peace from the inside out.

> "I think if we can come to every meal and take in every morsel with gratitude, there would be a huge shift."
>
> —Donna Collins, executive director of
> The Global Peace Project

Q: Donna, you are a woman of many passions, and one of them is conscious cooking. What do you think is the connection between food and world peace? How are they connected?

For me, food is a divine experience. God creates this food and somebody is going to prepare that food. Under normal circumstances, your mother starts off with giving you food from her body, and then she is the one who is generally preparing your food through the course of the day. Which kind of chicken soup, do you think, actually heals you better from a cold—the kind that comes from a can, the kind that comes from a restaurant, or the kind that your mother or your grandmother makes?

Q: *Mom's chicken soup is the best!*

It is the best. I believe this is the continuation of a divine flow. This is how love is expressed. In our country, the weight issues that people have are due to processed food. We're eating food that is not handmade or homemade. It's all full of chemicals. It's not from a conscious garden and not being made by your mother or your grandmother or your father or your husband or someone that puts effort into it as an expression of their affinity for you. For me, it's that kind of a thing. It's how I express how much I appreciate whoever comes into my home.

Q: *I love that idea of food being a way to receive the love and the care of the person that prepares it. You do some really interesting things when you prepare your foods. What are some of the rituals that you use when you're preparing food, to infuse it with that care and that love?*

We have a CD that has chants and songs of prayers from all over the world. They are very indigenous sounding, with lots of foot stomping and thumping. Someone asked me once, "Can you sing these for me?"

I said, "No, I don't even know the song!" I have no idea what they are singing. I just know that when I hear this music, it's part of my personal cooking experience and I'm just happy while I'm cooking. I think that affects the food.

When I was with Joe Dispenza (author of *Evolve Your Brain*), one of the concepts we discussed was the idea that if you ate a dozen doughnuts, and you understood mind-over-matter, the doughnuts wouldn't make you gain weight. That was always an intriguing thought to me. It's how we think about our food that makes the difference.

If you knew that everything that you put into your mouth was made by someone who is happy and joyful in their process, even if it was someone who works in a restaurant, to me that would mean a completely different thing. The molecular structure of that food would somehow be altered through the happiness of that person.

For me, the chants trigger happiness. I imagine that the whole world is in my kitchen when I am cooking, and I'm sort of stomping around, happily dancing and doing everything for everybody. That's where it starts.

Q: *Do you think you can taste the difference?*

We have done several home experiments, not scientific experiments. I have done things without the chants, rushed, trying to get it done as quickly as I can, forgetting in my rush to turn on the music, not taking off my shoes, just getting it out as quickly as I can. I used all the same ingredients, all organic, all good and healthy. And I've actually had my husband say, "You didn't make this, did you?"

It continues to freak me out. I look at him and say, "How could you tell?"

He can always pick out my cooking from a table of food by the way that it tastes. If I blindfolded him, he would be able to say, "Oh, you made this." He can always tell.

Q: *We have a ritual of blessing our food, which I think is something we often take for granted. Remember as kids when we would pray, "God is great. God is good. Let us thank Him for this food"? We have these blessings we would spit out as kids without really* *thinking about it. We knew at some level we were supposed to bless our food. But I think most of us aren't really conscious about it, even when we say the words. Hearing you talk about the joy and the dancing in preparing the food, it seems that blessing really is a significant act.*

I believe the blessing contributes to the happiness of the molecular structure of the food. Every molecule has the desire to fulfill its function. That may sound strange to some people, but I believe that a cup that is not being used is a very lonely cup. When something is in a state of disrepair, all those molecules are not being paid attention to. There is no observer to a broken item. One of the things that we know is that the observer is what holds matter together. In the process of blessing our food, it is more observed; therefore, it is more fulfilling of its function.

Q: Donna, I think of you as this cross between Betty Crocker and Mahatma Gandhi. You have this wonderful, happy, perky gift of cooking, and you also have a very strong vision of peace. You're bringing them both together in a way that's really delicious for people! What do you think someone like Gandhi would say about your mission to bring peace to the world by changing how we relate to our food?

I've cooked for his grandson, and the memory of having cooked for him seems to have stuck in his mind. I think that Gandhi would like the idea of breaking bread between different sides. Something happens in the process of breaking bread, physically breaking it and giving it to another person. We have common table manners from country to country. You pass the food after you take your portion. In every country, that is a common thing. You don't just slam the plate down, and let the person pick the plate up. You pass it to them. It's an unconscious thing.

But when you take a piece of bread, break off your portion, and pass it to the next person, to me that ritual in itself is a bonding experience.

One of the things we talked about with the Interfaith Peace Chapel here in Dallas is to have an event called "The Common Table" and call in people of all religions, every faith, every culture, and ask them to bring in a potluck item. Once a month, we would have a big, long, huge common table, where you're talking to people with every sort of difference, and seeing what it is you both like. Maybe it's the same dessert. It creates a common conversation. Maybe you're Jewish or maybe you're Muslim, but if you both like crème brûlée, that's a fun thing.

Q: That's right, some common ground!

Yes! We both like chocolate!

Q: We both like chocolate. There you go. We can start with that. What are some easy things that anybody can do to start bringing more peace into their diet?

The first thing is that you need to have at least one family meal a day where everyone is sitting down. There's no texting, no television, no computer. I don't care if it's only for 20 minutes. I don't even care even if it's just for part of that meal. When you sit down and you bless your food all at the same time, and everybody gets to say what happened to them during the day it creates a gathering point.

The second thing is that I am a World Peace Diet facilitator. For a very long time, being vegetarian has been a key component of all the things that I think are important. But I'm not suggesting that everyone be vegetarian. There are times when I eat meat and fish and those kinds of things, but I do want everybody to be really conscious. Even of the vegetables!

We need to raise our conscious awareness of how these things have come to our lives, and how they relate. Are you using clean food? Is it grass-fed, organic, free-range chicken, beef and those kinds of things? How is it being prepared?

Over the holidays, we were with a Jewish family. One of the women was explaining to me the importance of Kosher meat, which I had never really investigated. I started reading about it when I returned home.

When an animal is cowboyed, chased or hunted down, the amount of hormones that surges through the animal's body is actually detrimental when we eat it, and those hormones are all passed on to us. They are agitation hormones and adrenalin hormones. It's not a great thing for us to ingest.

Gandhi said, "The greatness of a nation and its moral progress can be judged by the ways its animals are treated." I do believe that these things have all been provided for us, and we should bless them in the process. If a human being gave up their life to protect us or do something for us, we would be holding that person in high esteem for the rest of our lives. When you're talking about animals, it's the same thing.

We have friends who are very involved in the First Nations community in Sedona. They said that buffalos have a contract with human beings to provide them with food, and that they have a closed herd in Sedona. They wanted me to try buffalo meat because they felt that it would be such a different experience for me, and I had never had it. They said that when they go to get a buffalo to turn it to meat, a buffalo will come out of the herd on its own and lay down.

Q: *Wow!*

There was one day when they went to get a buffalo, and a buffalo cow came out of the herd. Very quickly after that, her calf came running after her, and she took the calf and pushed him back into the herd. She came back again, and the calf wiggles out and came running after her again. Three times, the calf chased the mother cow. The third time, she pushed the calf back into the herd, and all of the other adult buffalos circled the calf and the mother went and lay down.

I hear those kinds of stories and I think, How can someone think that this is not about consciousness? They're giving up their lives for us. We should be good stewards of the earth by caring for them in humane ways. That is a big part of the message. That's co-creating.

Q: *If you could wave a magic wand, and change one thing about how the world or how America relates to food, or the things we eat, what would you want for people?*

I think if we can come to every meal and take in every morsel with gratitude, there would be a huge shift. Even eating fast food would be a different experience for us, because as a "fast food nation" part of what happens to us is that we eat without gratitude. That is a really big component. We must ask, "Can I take this into me with gratitude, for the hands that made it, for the animals that gave up their lives, for the plants that gave up their lives?"

To me that would be the biggest message that I could share: stop, take a breath before you take a bite, breathe into your heart and be grateful that you're in a nation that has the capacity to feed the world. We have enough food to feed the world here. If we can come from that state of gratitude, I think that it will shift a lot of things.

*****

Donna Collins has dedicated herself to helping people live more creative lives utilizing her incredible imagination and her exceptional culinary skills. Donna is a certified practitioner of HeartMath and EFT and was executive coordinator of the 2004 Gather the Women International Congress, which hosted 40 nonprofit organizations and United Nations partners from more than 20 countries. She continues to bring people together to create a shift in consciousness through her educational programs with The Global Peace Project (*www.theglobalpeaceproject.com*).

*****

Reflection Points

How conscious do you believe you are of the food you ingest from day to day?

What percentage of the meals you eat is prepared consciously? Can you taste the difference?

The Peacebuilder Challenge

With each meal this week, reflect upon the many people, animals and plants that are a part of putting that meal together. Before you eat, pause to give thanks for the farmers, the truck drivers and the grocery store clerks, as well as the animals and plants that are a part of the food itself.

21

BE THE CHANGE

Lisa Nichols

Lisa Nichols has been honored with many awards in recognition of her empowering work, including the Humanitarian Award from South Africa and the Ambassador of Good Will Award. A best-selling author, speaker and Law of Attraction teacher featured in the movie The Secret, *Lisa dedicates her life to service, philanthropy and healing. She shares with us a message of hope and possibility for infusing our lives with a profound and proactive spirit of peace.*

> "Peace is a verb. Peace is not just a noun. You do peace. You demonstrate it. You live it. You example it."
>
> —Lisa Nichols, *No Matter What!*

Q: Lisa, what do you believe is the power of collaboration?

When we begin to combine our energies, we will operate in a *flow* versus a *force* against one another. When I put my genius with your genius, we find a way to be in what I call *relay*.

I think *relay* is what relationships really are comprised of. It's you leaning towards me, me leaning towards you. We find flowing, expanding and contracting as necessary in the spirit of cooperation. But all of a sudden, we don't run against the resistance of one another. We move out of worry, doubt, scarcity, lack and deprivation. We move into abundance.

You and I can work in the same market, have the same consumer base, but because you have a different genius and I have a different genius, even if we're doing the same thing, we have different styles. If we find a way to operate an even flow with one another, we give our customer more. Our customer gets a greater value, and then we have greater peace and ease while operating in each other's space. So the power of cooperation versus competition is enormous.

Some of my best work has been done in the last year, because I've partnered with people who are in the same industry with me doing the exact same thing. We have a synergy with one another. My best work has been done with them beside me.

Q: Isn't it interesting? From the old mindset, it seems counterproductive; and yet, what we're finding is, like so many spiritual principles, it works. You had huge success with your book launch and that was a very collaborative effort, wasn't it?

My gosh, it was a huge collaborative effort. I went to all my friends who are in the business, who are in the industry, who sell books, who have their own books, who sell workshops. I said, "Let's partner!" They said, "Absolutely!" So we did exchanges all day long. They launched my book. I launched their book. They launched my products. I launched their products. It's a win-win.

In 37 days, *No Matter What!* hit six best-seller lists, including *The New York Times*, and it's already sold in 21 foreign languages. That is a result of cooperative work.

Q: Wow! This book, of course, is a collaborative project, bringing together amazing spiritual teachers and peacebuilders like you. Lisa, what does peace mean to you?

First, I am honored to be a part of this project. It brings my heart great healing, great love and great encouragement to know that I get to be a part of something bigger than all of us.

Peace, for me, means to move in the flow of God. Whatever you call your God: Mother, Father, God, Allah, Buddha, whatever. Our Higher Consciousness, our Higher Spirit, the God in each one of us is a God of peace and flow. It's when you can take that deep breath and feel that you're not resisting anything. Nor are you trying to push anything. You have peace.

I think of a braid with three strands woven together. When you braid something, it's always stronger. I think that the braid of peace is the you and the I. It's the man and the woman. It's the black and the white. It's the Christian and the Buddhist. It's all of us being able to come together to honor our differences, celebrate our likenesses and to combine our energy of love so we can make something greater than each one of us could ever be individually.

When I braid and fold the fabric of me together with the fabric of you, and we flow in the spirit of peace, there is strength. There is humility. There is grace. There is celebration. There is a power that cannot exist without that braid.

Peace for me means that we move in the flow of God. We move in the flow of the rhythm, the river. We are the navigation of the universe. We are not operating on our own agenda. We are operating on a universal agenda.

When I was on the way to South Africa, I read the press release of what I was supposed to do when I got there. I assumed I was going to talk about *The Secret* because that's what everyone would call me for. I just thought, Let me just peruse the press release. It's a 15-hour flight. Why not?

The press release said, "Lisa Nichols will come to help heal our cultural wounds of the past." I've never done anything like that. Only in that moment did I realize that I was bringing together the Africans and Afrikaners for the first time in this group of people.

The black people and the white people in South Africa would never talk because of apartheid, but I was given the assignment to bring peace to this part of the world. I'd never done anything like that. So for the next 14 1/2 hours, I prayed.

What I had to do in order to bring that to them was find and center myself in peace, center myself at our likeness, celebrate and honor our differences, and find the place where we all flow like the river and celebrate the God in each one of us.

By the time I landed, I was at a whole other level of consciousness because literally for 14 1/2 hours I was in prayer mode to deliver something I'd never brought forth before. When you experience a sense of peace in a place that hasn't had it before, it's the sweet nectar of the world. It is the sweetest nectar that we could ever taste.

Q: Yes. I think many of us are feeling called into being of service in a way we have never been called before. What you're saying is so profound: It is prayer that lifts our consciousness so that we may do those things that we're getting called to do.

Absolutely. In this stage of my life, I pray for every season. I say, "God, what am I supposed to be doing in this season? Tell me how I'm supposed to be in service." In this season, it's to teach what it means to live in peace, and to live in flow and fluidity, versus in resistance and force.

Do you realize the power of internal peace? When I have internal peace with the fact that I was touched inappropriately; when I have internal peace with the fact that I wasn't an A student but a C student; when I have internal peace with my mocha skin and my full lips; when I have internal peace with the extra 30 pounds that I brought along the way; when I have internal peace with the greatness and the giant that God gave me inside of me; when I have peace with all of that, then I get to bring to you a peaceful me and we get to create a peaceful us. Then we get to touch and help to design a peaceful planet.

So my season now is about helping people find their core strength, their humility and their peace within. Those are literally the trainings that I'm doing now just because that's the season. It's that important that God had said, "I want you to focus on what peace looks like internally so that we can now give peace externally to others and show them. Demonstrate it."

Q: Your book No Matter What! *speaks about the mindset of commitment. How do we take that "no-matter-what" ideology into the peace movement? What does that look like?*

You would be willing to live and demonstrate it personally. That's number one. We don't force anyone to do anything. We be. We be it. You be it. And I mean it that way for all of you grammar experts. I mean it that way.

You be it. Then you allow it to ooze from your essence so that it becomes contagious to others. Do you realize that your love, your peace, your joy, your bliss can be so powerful in you that it becomes contagious, and people just want to be around you and they don't even know why? They want to follow you. They want to be your Facebook friends. They want to Tweet with you. They don't know why.

But see, if you're being that essence and then you speak about it, you talk about it, you walk about it, you live it, you breathe it, you walk it, you talk it, you sing it, you drink it, then when you sweat, it comes from your pores, girl!

That's when you're steeped in it. You're steeped in possibility. You're steeped in reverence. You're steeped in humility. You're steeped in grace.

Every day I walk for about an hour and no one comes anywhere within 20 feet of me without me saying, "Hello. How are you?" Now I've got to tell you, I catch some people off guard. They probably think I'm very strange and that's okay. But I'm going to show you love.

I'm going to show you love no matter what. My love isn't contingent on you loving me. My love for you isn't contingent on you being nice to me. My love isn't contingent on the economics being right on the planet. My love is my love and I'm going to give it fluently and freely. I'm going to show you what it feels like to give with no expectations. I'm going to give crazy. I'm going to love crazy. That's how you do it.

Q: *That sounds like fun.*

I get so excited. I get excited talking about it because it's dancing to your own rhythm and it's dancing to the rhythm of the universe. It's saying, "God, I hear You. I feel You. I am with You and I am going to be the demonstration for Your children." You know what I mean?

Here's the key thing: You can't be rocked or rattled by what's going on around you because if you're waiting for the economy to get right, you're waiting for people around you to show up before you do peace, before you do love, before you do crazy love and crazy peace, you're going to be waiting awhile. Honey, you're going to waiting for a while.

You are the heart beating. You are the essence. You are the seed that's already cultivated. You are the seed. I love this. I heard this from Dr. Beckwith yesterday: "You're the seed with the tree in it already." Can you imagine?

You're the rose seed with the rose bush in it already. The rose bush is already in the seed. The tree is already in the seed. You are the seed. You are planted. You are planted right here on this place called Earth.

Be the tree. Do you know? I'm so excited.

Q: *Yes, absolutely. I do, too, because I think people hear "Peace Movement" and think back to the old days of protest and fighting against something. That's not at all what we're talking about here. I think the consciousness has expanded to a level where a new paradigm for peacebuilding is emerging.*

We also think it might be sitting with your arms crossed and meditating for 40 hours a day. It doesn't mean that either. It means meditation. It means being centered. It means being connected to a Higher Source. It means that.

But it also means wake up. Jump up. Play. Play full out. Love full out. Embrace full out. Listen to this: *Forgive full out.*

It is as active as it is not. It's not about fighting against something, but it's also not about sitting, saying, "I'm in peace so I'm going to sit under this tree for the next 17 years and just wait for it all to occur around me." No!

It's about being in the game, playing full out. This is about being that demonstration of what's possible. It's about being a demonstration of forgiveness. It's about being that demonstration of trusting and having unwavering faith, leaping off the ledge of your life, knowing that either God is going to give you wings to fly or God is going to give you something really, really soft to land on. It's about operating like that too.

Peace is as active as it is passive. Does that make sense?

Peace is a verb. Peace is not just a noun. You do peace. You demonstrate it. You live it. You example it.

You don't just example it when everything is going wonderful. You example it in the middle of chaos. You example it and exude peace.

I was just walking with my walking partner this morning and she said, "My husband and I were talking about you yesterday, and we have a question for you."

I said, "What?"

She goes, "Are you always this happy? How do you always stay this happy?"

Then she went on and asked me—this is really cute—she goes, "Are you just born that way?"

I said, "Laura, if I told you I was born this way, that would let you off the hook." She was silent. I said, "I'm not going to let you off the hook, sweetie. This is a choice." She was silent and then I was silent, which was more powerful than anything I could have said. I let her think about that.

No, I wasn't born this way. I choose to be a demonstration and there are days I have to remind myself: Get back into your Higher Consciousness, Lisa. Operate on the level that God put you on, not on your human, physical level where you get a little nervous, or a little *school is starting and my son goes to a private school—my gosh, that means mega-tuition.* Okay, great. That's my human part wandering.

My Higher Conscious part says, "It is all done, honey. It is all done." Do you know what I mean?

Q: Yes, and that brings up a good point because I know your passion is working with young people. You talk about being a demonstration of peace. What can we do to be role models for peace for this emerging generation? How can we help our young people?

Take bigger risks with them. Let them see the woman and the man, not just the mother and the father. Show them.

Read my book and watch the level of discomfort I must have had to share that level of truth with you, then be willing to share that level of truth with someone that's between the ages of 12 and 25. Be willing to let them see who you are on the journey. That's number one.

Number two, show unconditional love. That means love them through their ugly. When it's difficult, start with the words, "I love you, and we're going to get through this." Show them that you're going to be there even through their dark years, if they should have them, and then show no judgment. Show no judgment when they make a mistake.

You may have to correct them, but show no judgment. Judgment makes us afraid to open up. We don't feel it's safe, so make it safe.

Go to *www.lisa-nichols.com.* Click on *Motivating the Teen Spirit* and see the video. Then recreate that experience in your life and the lives of your children.

Q: *Lisa, if there were one piece of advice you would give people who are maybe not in such a peaceful environment/outer world, who are seeking the peace that you're been talking about, that dance of love, that dance of joy, what advice would you give them?*

I would say, every day, stand in the mirror. Complete three sentences looking at yourself:

Say "I am proud that you_____." Celebrate yourself.

Say "I forgive you for _____." Release yourself of any old worries and doubts.

Then say, "I commit to you that _____."

Every day, celebrate yourself. Forgive yourself. And commit to yourself something new before you introduce yourself to the world. Give them the best you possible.

Thank you, Mindy, for celebrating with me, and thank you for allowing me to celebrate with you. I believe in everything you are working for and standing for. I'm with you. I am your sister in the journey.

*****

Lisa Nichols (*www.lisa-nichols.com*) is one of the featured teachers from the hit movie and best-selling book *The Secret.* She is the author of *No Matter What!: 9 Steps to Living the Life You Love.* In addition, Lisa is the founder of Motivating the Masses and CEO of Motivating the Teen Spirit, LLC. Her transformational workshops have impacted the lives of more than 210,000 teens and over 1 million adults.

*****

Reflection Points

What do you celebrate about yourself?

In what ways are you/could you be a role model to the young people in your community?

The Peacebuilder Challenge

Stand in front of your mirror each day for the next seven days and follow Lisa's suggestion of completing these sentences:

I am proud that you _____.

I forgive you for _____.

I commit to you that _____.

Let It Begin With Me

Mindy Audlin

> We shall not cease from exploration
> And the end of all our exploring
> Will be to arrive where we started
> And know the place for the first time.
>
> —T.S. Eliot, *Four Quartets*

As I reflect on the wealth of wisdom represented by the 21 visionary leaders who contributed to this project, I am struck by three major observations:

First, it is apparent how the commitment of even a small group of people can make a radical difference on our planet. In boardrooms and living rooms, through spiritual practice and community initiatives, people around the world are bringing the consciousness of peace to their passions. And it does make a difference.

Secondly, I am struck by the awareness of how many people are working together alongside each of our 21 featured leaders to turn the vision of peace into a daily reality. As you will see in the resource section that follows, for each person who shared their perspective, there are teams of people working behind the scenes with equal passion and commitment, dedicated to doing what they feel called and inspired to do.

But perhaps the most significant *aha!* from these interviews for me is the realization that multitudes of people, people like you and me, can integrate the insights and philosophies of the interviewees into our lives. We can create new habits. We can see with new eyes. And we can change.

And every time we do, every time we shift from judgment to love, every time we refuse to be entertained by violence, every time we buy organic produce and meat products certified as part of a humane program, we bring our world a little more back into balance. Inch by inch, we return to our natural state of peace and grace. Choice by choice. Person by person.

This is our great call to action.

My prayer is that, as you reach the end of this book, you begin a new way of approaching the moments that make up your life. May this ending signal the beginning of a new era of peace in your own heart. And may the ripples of that peace be cause for celebrating every living being on our glorious planet Earth.

*****

Reflection Points

Reflect on your activities through the Peacebuilder Challenges throughout this book. What have you learned through them? How have they impacted your life?

What "aha" moments did *you* have based on these interviews?

The Peacebuilder Challenge

Create a sustainable plan for moving forward as a peacebuilder. Choose at least one action or process from this book to put into an ongoing sustainable peace practice.

RESOURCES

Chapter 1

The Institute of Heartmath: *www.heartmath.org*

The Global Coherence Initiative: *www.glcoherence.org*

Chapter 2

Barbara Marx Hubbard and the Foundation for Conscious Evolution:

www.barbaramarxhubbard.com

Global Family: *www.globalfamily.net*

Hummingbird Living School:

www.hummingbirdlivingschool.org

Lynne Twist / The Pachamama Alliance: *www.pachamama.org*

Suggested Reading

The Eye of the I by Dr. David Hawkins

Emergence: The Shift From Ego to Essence by Barbara Marx Hubbard

Chapter 3

Edgar Mitchell, Apollo 14 Astronaut:

www.edmitchellapollo14.com/

The Institute of Noetic Sciences: *www.noetic.org*

Care2.com: *www.care2.com/greenliving/*

Chapter 4

Stephen Dinan: *www.stephendinan.com*

Lawrence Ellis: *www.LawrenceEllis.org www.PathstoChange.net*

The Summer of Peace: *www.summerofpeace.net*

The Shift in Action Partners Program: *www.shiftinaction.com*

The Shift Network, Inc.: *www.theshiftnetwork.com*

Challenge Day: *www.challengeday.org*

It Gets Better Project: *www.itgetsbetter.org*

Generation Five: *www.generationfive.org*

The United Nations Convention on the Elimination of all forms of Discrimination Against Women: *www.un.org/women watch/daw/cedaw*

The International Council of Thirteen Indigenous Grandmothers: *www.grandmotherscouncil.org*

The Urban Peace Movement: *www.urbanpeacemovement.org*

The Department of Peace: *www.thepeacealliance.org*

The National Peace Academy: *www.nationalpeaceacademy.us/*

Take the Vow of Nonviolence: *www.itakethevow.com*

Van Jones: *www.vanjones.net/*

Art in Action: *www.artinactionworld.org/*

Spirit Rock Meditation Center: *www.spiritrock.org /*

Where the Hell Is Matt? *www.wherethehellismatt.com/*

YourCause: *www.yourcause.com*

Chapter 5

The Palyul Lineage of Tibetan Buddhism: *www.palyul.org*

Chapter 6

The Demartini Institute: *www.drdemartini.com*

Suggested Reading

From Stress to Success in Just 31 Days by Dr. John Demartini

Chapter 7

CEO SPACE: *www.ceospace.net*

CEO SPACE NATION: *www.ceospacenation.com*

Chapter 8

Joe Vitale: *www.joevitale.com* or *www.mrfire.com*

Operation YES: *www.operationyes.com*

Move the Mountain: *www.movethemountain.org*

Suggested Reading

The Secret by Rhonda Byrne

Zero Limits by Dr. Joe Vitale and Ihaleakala Hew Len

The Attractor Factor by Joe Vitale

Attract Money Now by Joe Vitale:

Chapter 9

The Universe Lies Within: *www.theuniverselieswithin.com*

What the BLEEP Do We Know? *www.whatthebleep.com*

Emotional Freedom Technique (EFT): *www.eftuniverse.com*

Suggested Reading

The Conscious Universe by Dean Radin

Scientific Research on Maharishi's Transcendental Meditation and TM-Sidhi Programme: Collected Papers, Volume 4, pp. 2623-2634. Vlodrop, The Netherlands: Maharishi Vedic University Press, 1989.

Chapter 10

Silent Unity 24/7 Prayer Support: 800-NOW-PRAY (800-669-7729) or

www.silentunity.org

World Day of Prayer: *www.worlddayofprayer.org*

Chapter 11

Unity Worldwide Ministries: *www.unity.org/association*

BePeace™: *www.rasurinternational.org*

www.academyforpeacecr.org

Soles4Souls: *www.soles4souls.org*

Chapter 12

The Blackson Group: *www.kuteblackson.com*

Chapter 13

Azim Khamisa: *www.azimkhamisa.com*

The Tariq Khamisa Foundation (TKF): *www.tkf.org*
Suggested Reading
The Secrets of the Bulletproof Spirit: How to Bounce Back From Life's Hardest Hits by Azim Khamisa and Jillian Quinn

Chapter 14

Andrew Harvey: *www.andrewharvey.net*
Institute for Sacred Activism:
www.instituteforsacredactivism.com
Suggested Reading
The Hope: A Guide to Sacred Activism by Andrew Harvey

Chapter 15

The Global Alliance for Transformational Entertainment (GATE): *www.gatecommunity.org*
The Visioneering Group: *www.thevisioneeringgroup.com*
Better U Foundation: *www.betterufoundation.org*
Suggested Reading
The Power of Now by Eckhart Tolle

Chapter 16

Thomas P.M. Barnett's Blog: *www.thomasbarnett.com*
The Friendship Force: *www.thefriendshipforce.org*
Suggested Reading
Great Powers: America and the World After Bush by Thomas P.M. Barnett (2009)
Blueprint for Action: A Future Worth Creating by Thomas P.M. Barnett (2005)
The Pentagon's New Map: War and Peace in the Twenty-First Century by Thomas P.M. Barnett (2004)

Chapter 17

Intent.com: *www.intent.com*

Suggested Reading
100 Promises to My Baby by Mallika Chopra:
www.babypromises.com

Chapter 18

Wendy Craig-Purcell: *www.wendycraigpurcell.com*
The Unity Center: *www.theunitycenter.net*
The Association for Global New Thought (AGNT):
www.agnt.org
Suggested Reading
Ask Yourself This: Questions to Open the Heart, Expand the Mind and Awaken the Soul by Wendy Craig-Purcell

Chapter 19

Jim Bunch: *www.jimbunch.com*
The Ultimate Game of Life (TUG):
www.theultimategameoflife.com

Chapter 20

The Global Peace Project: *www.theglobalpeaceproject.com*
Dr. Joe Dispenza: *www.drjoedispenza.com*
The Interfaith Peace Chapel: *interfaithpeacechapel.org*
Gather the Women: *www.gatherthewomen.org*
Suggested Reading
The World Peace Diet: worldpeacediet.org

Chapter 21

Lisa Nichols: *www.lisa-nichols.com*
Motivating the Teen Spirit: *www.motivatingtheteenspirit.com*
Suggested Reading
No Matter What! 9 Steps to Living the Life You Love by Lisa Nichols

Additional Resource

The Unity Online Radio Network: *www.unity.fm*

ACKNOWLEDGEMENTS

It was an ambitious goal, to be sure: Bring together some of the greatest luminaries of our time. Interview them. Transcribe it. Edit it. Write a book. Create a website. Align with like-minded organizations. And ultimately bring the message and the consciousness of peace to people around the world.

I pulled together a team and we set our sights on September 21, International Day of Peace. We had 12 weeks to pull it all together. I'd like to thank everyone who volunteered their time and talent to make this project a success.

Special thanks to Data Process Outsourcing, Inc. (*www.dataprocess.org*) for taking on the task of transcribing our interviews. I appreciate your generous spirit and your professional quality work!

Thank you to Donna Collins and Bruce Yamini (and team!) for your help at every stage of the project and for spending countless hours sifting through rough interviews and putting them into an easy-to-read format.

Thank you to the spiritual dynamos at Unity Online Radio for providing the platform for these interviews and to Unity Books for giving it new and expanded life in its current book form.

And of course, thank you to my beloved husband and daughter for your patience as I poured myself into yet another life-consuming passion. You are my anchor. I am so blessed to have you in my life.

ABOUT THE AUTHOR

Mindy Audlin brings the power of possibility to people around the world. The author of *What If It All Goes Right? Creating a New World of Peace, Prosperity and Possibility* and *Let It Begin With Me: 21 Voices of the New Peace Movement,* Mindy helps individuals and organizations use spiritual principles that create a tangible shift in real-world results.

Mindy was the founding Spiritual Leader for Unity Church of Wimberley, Texas, and the founder of Unity Online Radio, where she interviewed many of the most influential spiritual teachers and thought leaders of our time, including Eckhart Tolle, Deepak Chopra, Marianne Williamson and Byron Katie through her weekly program *The Leading Edge.*

As the founder of Network on Purpose (*www.networkonpurpose.com*), Mindy currently helps purpose-driven entrepreneurs fulfill their calling by tapping into an innovative community of peers, experts and business-building resources.

Mindy is a charismatic public speaker, engaging facilitator and a dynamic spiritual teacher. To learn more about booking Mindy for a corporate event, keynote, workshop or retreat, visit *www.mindyaudlin.com.*